The Essential Television Handbook

What you need to know, what to do and what not to do

For Producers, Directors, Researchers, PAs,
Production Managers, Location Managers,
and Television Journalists

Peter Jarvis

Focal Press
An Imprint of Butterworth-Heinemann
Linacre House, Jordan Hill, Oxford OX2 8DP
225 Wildwood Avenue, Woburn MA 01801-2041
A division of Reed Educational and Professional Publishing Ltd

 A member of the Reed Elsevier plc group

OXFORD AUCKLAND BOSTON
JOHANNESBURG MELBOURNE NEW DELHI

First published 1996
Transferred to digital printing 2001

British Library Cataloguing in Publication Data
A catalogue record for this book is available from the British Library

Library of Congress Cataloguing in Publication Data
A catalogue record for this book is available from the Library of Congress

ISBN 0 240 51444 9

For information on all Focal Press publications
visit our website at www.focalpress.com

CONTENTS

INTRODUCTION

Finding a title for this book has not been easy. 'Sod's Law' initially suggested itself. A full thirty years in broadcasting has convinced me that if something can go wrong it probably will. A second stab was 'Another Fine Mess You've Gotten Us In', the catchphrase cry of Oliver Hardy to Stan Laurel. But it seemed unwise to assume that all our readers would be film buffs or get the reference. The final choice of title is neither dramatic nor eye-catching but at least accurately describes what the book sets out to convey.

The transformation of television over the past decade has been extraordinary and the revolutionary changes show no sign of slackening pace. The recent politics of television have been driven by a mixture of political dogma, breakneck technological advance and financial conniving at national and international levels. Only ancients like myself can fondly remember when all British television was either the mighty BBC, which represented the ideal of Public Service Broadcasting, or the regionally based commercial TV companies, which shared much the same ethos and were heavily infiltrated by BBC-trained staff. Staffing levels, working conditions, pay and promotion were policed by powerful trades unions, particularly in the ITV companies. For those who wanted it, television could offer a lifetime career.

All that has been blown away. In the successive waves of deregulation the ITV companies have engaged in a series of mergers and cross-shareholding deals which pessimists suggest may leave only one or two companies owning all terrestrial broadcast TV by the beginning of the new millennium. And as the domestic scene only mirrors the international, the final winners may not be British. Companies like Time Warner, Disney and Rupert Murdoch's News International bestride the airwaves of the world.

The trades unions are shadows of their former selves. In any case the majority of the ITV companies are no longer major programme makers but see themselves as publishers. The pattern has been followed by the BBC, which has been ruthlessly shedding production and service staff (though notably not accountants and managers) whilst farming out 25 per cent of its production, under Government instruction, to outsiders. It would be an optimistic young man or woman today who looked to any television company for the prospect of a steady job, let alone a lifelong career.

The prospects for faster and faster technological change makes any prediction about the future as certain as a win on the National Lottery. At the end of 1995 the Government awarded the franchise for a fifth national terrestrial television channel. All the terrestrial broadcasters pin their hopes on a leap into digital transmission, which will immeasurably improve the technical quality of the programmes as well as adding to the numbers of terrestrial channels. But the success of digital transmissions will depend on persuading, or forcing, the public to buy new receivers.

The tempting prospect of wide-screen television has been on the horizon so long that it seems like a permanent mirage. As with so much technological advance where do you stop and risk enormous capital expenditure on one system when there is always something better in the pipeline? Here is the familiar chicken and egg dilemma. How do you persuade the viewers to rush out and buy utterly new technology before cheap receivers and the prospect of new programmes in the new format are available? Most viewers seem quite satisfied with horribly ill-adjusted home receivers and dismal quality VHS cassettes.

Wild-eyed techno freaks who envisage a prospect of wafer-thin wall-sized television screens with access to uncountable digital wide-screen interactive channels might consider this. The pace setters, Japan and the USA, are still saddled with the 50 year old 525 line transmission system NTSC which initials are commonly taken by Europeans to mean Never Twice The Same Colour. All this may become irrelevant in light of the steadily increasing power of the new boys on the block, cable and satellite. As town after town is supplied with cable, there is the prospect of telephone companies carrying television and cable television companies carrying telephone lines and the whole lot involved in computer networks. Interactive systems and video-on-demand are around the corner. Cyberspace and the Information Superhighway may be set to change the world or may be not. Human nature is obstinate. Research findings presented to the British Association for the Advancement of Science meeting in 1995 suggested that over 50 per cent of Internet hits by university students were in search of pornography.

Enough of the present background. By the time this book reaches your hands, Dear Reader, it will be out of date. The concern here is to address the people who at the end of the day they all depend on. All the politicians, and accountants and advertisers and tycoons and manufacturers and cyberspace evangelists, depend on there somewhere being an army of creative foot soldiers who can make the programmes that people will want to watch.

The need is there. Annual UK licensed transmission hours doubled between 1990 and 1995. Twenty-four hours a day broad-casting has become normal. The conservative forecast is that these hours will treble again by the year 2000 as more channels come on stream. There is the horrid prospect of many of these channels doing no more than carry repeats of ancient American sit-coms or obscure sports supported by tacky local advertising. But to succeed, the new stations will have to provide perceptible amounts of original programming. A number of UK cable channels already offer up to 40 per cent original material. They may have no choice in future. The European Union (EU), pushed largely by the French government, is consideringa minimum quota of 50 per cent original material for European cable services. An EU directive, Television without Frontiers, is currently under discussion and if agreed by the European Parliament will oblige all stations to invest 15 per cent of their annual turnover in 'European Product'. All of this adds up to an awful lot of new programmes to fill up an awful lot of new air time.

Unfortunately there is not an awful lot of new money available. The most optimistic estimate is for a growth in broadcasting revenue of only 50 per cent over the coming five years. In real terms companies like the BBC may see no income growth at all. And instead of growing the figures for television viewing hours are static or even in decline. The average UK viewer watches around 3.5 hours a day, much the same as five years ago.

One of the immediate consequences for today's new entrants will be multi-skilling. Cable companies and even BBC Worldwide have already introduced the Hi-8 camera-toting video journalist and the one-man news/current affairs camera crew is widely established. The disk cameras soon to appear may combine with desktop editing systems and reduce cheap programmes to one-man or one-woman shows.

The ambitious new entrant to the industry may have in mind the prospect of working on one of the brilliant drama series that only British television seems capable, still, of creating. Or maybe ambition points to the stunning documentaries that distinguish still the BBC and Channel 4, or hard-hitting current affairs investigative television journalism.

The humdrum reality though is more and more space to be filled for less and less money and longer working hours for less reward. The management guru, Sir John Harvey Jones, has suggested that the only reason for working in television is the attractive lifestyle; forget the prospect of making money.

The British Film Institute is conducting a Television Industry Tracking Study and has published an interim report. It shows ever fewer full-time jobs and an ever-expanding cottage industry of independent production companies. At the same time there is a flood of new recruits desperately knocking at the door. There has been a boom in academic courses variously called Media Studies, Film Studies or Communication Studies. Once an academic curiosity of no importance to a real job, Media Studies has become the first step for around a quarter of those now entering television.

But there is still the entrenched view that a qualification in Media Studies no more prepares a graduate for the practicalities of programme making than a degree in Military History trains one to ride a horse.

In the past, real training began on the job with the first appointment and lasted a lifetime. There was little formal production training except by the BBC and, even there, progress was effectively by apprenticeship. Assistant cameramen, assistant film editors and assistant producers rose slowly to become full cameramen, editors and producers. PAs and film clerks were promoted by stages to vision mixers and to directors and beyond. At every level the recruit was watched, advised and protected from disaster by experienced colleagues and supported by companies of service staff from music librarians and designers to copyright lawyers and shipping agents.

Today it ain't necessarily so.

There is no less creative talent available now than at any earlier time. What is lacking is the framework for nurturing and developing it effectively. The industry now has skillset whose brief is to establish and administer sets of National Vocational Qualifications. Ideally a new entrant, condemned to a career of short-term contracts and regular changes of employer, might be able to collect a series of NVQs as expertise and seniority grows. The success of NVQs will still depend on how seriously employers take them as qualifications. The British Film Institute shows that 38 per cent of the 21–30 year old age band in the industry got their first breaks through a personal contact. In a fragmenting business where personal networking is the way to get jobs and nepotism has always been important, NVQs may have a hard time becoming the lodestone of the industry. I hope though that this handbook will be an important introductory guide for those setting out to climb this particular ladder.

There are libraries of books analysing films frame by frame and scripts line by line, not including the countless erudite works on the semiology of the screen, racial and sexual stereotyping, violence, delinquency, viewing patterns by social class and so on. The author would not wish to add to them. There exists also a small number of handbooks on the practical skills of directing and producing or the specialist areas of research or programme management. But as far as I know there is no book which has tried to pull together the wide ranging subject areas which every programme maker must be familiar with if a creative career is not going to be marked by a trail of chaos.

Any programme maker is going to come up against problems of copyright. Every location is fraught with practical difficulties. Any decision involving contributors raises problems of contracts, conditions and health and safety. To be original and creative is not enough. Television is about saving time and money, keeping to budget, hitting deadlines and making the best of what is available. All of which involves knowing where the problems are coming from and not being taken by surprise by them. This cannot be a textbook. Nobody knows all there is to be known about subjects like copyright or defamation nor would it serve any purpose to spell out in detail the agreements between television companies and the Musicians' Union or every relevant paragraph of the Health and Safety at Work Act.

But anyone plunging into television production ought at least to be aware of the pitfalls that underlie any of these subject areas. And if there is no immediate advisor available the programme maker ought to know of some body or some organisation to contact for help. Unlike the happy few joining big companies on secure contracts the independent beginner can be frighteningly alone if things go wrong. I would like then to hope that this short handbook lives up to its title and is an essential guide to the practicalities of making television programmes for absolute beginners and a handy reference for those already established in the industry.

It would be invidious to try to offer individual thanks to any of the dozens of individuals and organisations who have helped in the production of this book. I would just like to offer general thanks to the staff of PACT, the BBC, the British and Regional Film Commissions and the many guilds and associations mentioned in the text who have put up with my persistent worrying, as often as not by telephone and fax and at inconvenient times.

I have tried to follow my own advice and where I have not had an answer I have turned to someone qualified. Anecdotal matter and tendentious opinions are all my responsibility as are any unwarranted generalisations or errors of fact. I can think of no reason why Sod's Law, which lies in wait for all programme makers, should not also apply to those who have the temerity to give them advice.

Peter Jarvis

Those working in television production are represented by these two professional associations, the one covering mainly broadcast work, the other mainly the corporate and training areas. There are a number of professional bodies representing specialist interests which are referred to in the text.

PACT (Producers' Alliance for Cinema and Television)
Gordon House
Greencoat Place,
London SW1P 1PH

IVCA (International Visual Communications Association)
Bolsover House
5–6 Clipstone Street
London W1V 3RD

For comprehensive information about the many organisations, companies and services alluded to in the text, readers should refer either to

The Knowledge (Miller Freeman Technical Ltd, Tonbridge, Kent)

or to

Kemps Film, TV and Video Handbook (Reed Information Services, East Grinstead, West Sussex)

1

ON LOCATION

Public and private

Production crews on location are pests. They occupy other people's property, they take up other people's time, they disrupt other people's lives. However it is likely that locations will be available on sufferance or in return for cash. So the choice of locations, where a choice exists, is crucial to the success of a programme.

It is an old legal gag that it is impossible to appear in a public place without risking arrest. If you stand still you are causing an obstruction, if you ask the time of day you may be begging or soliciting, if you stroll slowly you may be loitering with intent and if you run you may risk causing a breach of the peace. None of this legal nonsense is likely to bother the honest citizen about everyday business. But an unprepared crew at large may easily find that the courtroom joke is founded on some serious reality. All locations, whether on public land or privately owned property, present their special problems.

Public property and the police

There is in the UK no centralised system of accreditation for crews nor is permission to shoot in public places automatically needed. Although some kind or accreditation or press card can come in very useful it is not a requirement. Police commissioners have no authority to issue permits for shooting and under normal circumstances they will not try to prevent it. On the other hand the UK is a long way behind a city like New York where a detachment of police is permanently assigned to assisting visiting film and television companies. A move to remedy this is the recent setting up of regional film commissions, which can help liaise with the police and the whole range of official organisations, but their real priority is to act as facilitators for major productions and in particular for foreign ones. The producers of more modest and local location shoots have to work things out for themselves.

With any production involving more than a few hand-held shots, it pays to notify the local police station in advance. In many areas the relevant officer will probably do no more than pass the information about your presence to the local beat officer or patrol car; in others though, such as some central London areas, you may be asked to give details of your shooting plans and may expect a visit during the day. And if your project is of a scale requiring the setting up of lights or blocking off of parking bays then you are advised to write to the Chief Inspector (Operations) of the local police station or stations in whose area you intend to shoot. You will be expected to give a minimum of one week's notice.

The police are not there to stop you filming. They are there to stop you breaking the law or conducting yourself in a way likely to provoke others to break it. Each force may have its own guidelines but the following is a fair résumé of their normal requirements.

- If the police on duty tell you to stop filming you must do so. Refusal to do so may count as the criminal offence of Obstructing a Police Officer in Pursuit of His Duty. You will not be told to stop without good reason.
- There can be no enactment of a street crime or public disturbance without proper consultation and the presence of police officers. You will usually be expected to notify local businesses and residents in advance. The emergency services do not want to have calls from members of the public panicked by your brilliantly impersonated bank raid. Nor do you want a public-spirited individual to attack your fleeing mugger, as happened once in one of the author's productions.
- It is an offence to impersonate a police officer or member of the armed services. So actors in police costume should as far as possible remove caps and cover their uniforms between takes. They certainly must not be allowed to wander into the local pub in full costume.
- It is forbidden to fit flashing lights, horns or sirens to imitation police cars. If you need to shoot a sequence on a public highway you must dub on the effects later.
- Imitation firearms must be kept concealed from the public (see Chapter 9).
- No filming is permitted which contravenes the Road Traffic Acts, which rules out car chases, driving the wrong way down one-way streets, etc. Using prop vehicles in public places opens a whole new can of worms (see pp. 43–44).
- Parking dispensation cannot be arranged by the police. If

there is a requirement to assign parking bays or suspend any other highway regulations it is up to the production company to negotiate with the relevant local highway authority. This will probably involve paying a fee, and evidence of the relevant permission must be presented to the police on duty if requested.

• The production must avoid obstructing public thoroughfares with cables, lights or camera mounts. In the case of night shoots care must be taken that glaring lights are not a hazard to traffic or a nuisance to local residents.

• If the production is large enough to require a police presence for traffic or crowd control then the company must apply for the special services of the police to be supplied and these will have to be paid for.

• The filming is entirely the responsibility of the production company and all liabilities are its own, regardless of any police cooperation.

Even if you are confident that you are going to do nothing in contravention of these basic police requirements, you must still consider whether your actions are going to antagonise the ordinary public.

An ordinary tripod on a busy pavement constitutes an obstruction. Directors and reporters can offend owners and customers by blocking off shop and office entrances. Recordists may insist that workmen stop machines or turn off transistor radios during takes. Crews regularly demand that pedestrians do not walk through shot but sometimes leave them with the choices of turning awkward, hanging about waiting, or stepping off the pavement into the path of the next bus.

Never forget that the camera acts like a magnet to some people. Drunks and beggars have long since learned how to pester crews and obstruct shots as a sure way to extort payment to go away or to shut up. Objectionable teenagers just love to creep into the background of shots to wave and make obscene gestures. More seriously, in some inner city areas the past use of cameras by the police and social services have made all television crews suspect. If things start getting out of hand you might be grateful for a little police support but you are less likely to get it if you have not notified the local station in the first place. In fact if your presence creates crowds, causes a nuisance or provokes protest, you are yourselves liable for arrest for Conduct Likely to Cause a Breach of the Peace.

Private security

As location crews have become more and more prone to random intimidation and, more frequently, petty theft, a number of private security firms now offer the services of show guards to act as drivers, bodyguards and guardians of those tempting shiny aluminium flight cases in the back of the camera car.

Note though:

- Private security guards have no police powers or special dispensation. They are employees of the production team, nothing more.
- Professional bona fides need to be checked. A national television company was severely embarrassed at one Notting Hill Carnival when its own minders were arrested for carrying offensive weapons.
- The production company remains responsible for the health and safety of its security staff, the same as any other crew members. PACT has passed on to its members a warning from the Health and Safety Executive complaining about security guards being kept on duty for up to 48 hours at a time with no provision for meal breaks, rest or washing and toilet facilities.

There are certain definite prohibitions, particularly in London. There are tight restrictions on unauthorised filming around Westminster and Whitehall when Parliament is sitting and also around Buckingham Palace. You must be very careful about shooting in the vicinity of any law courts which are in session.

Private property

By now you have probably decided that if possible you should shoot on private property.

This is probably just as well since a great deal of the property generally thought of as public does in fact have a private owner. Very few spaces apart from the highway are genuinely public. Most parks and public gardens and many city squares are private and to use them you ought to ask permission and in many cases pay a fee. Of course many news and current affairs crews have taken the attitude that they have neither the time nor the inclination to bother with trivial formalities and the worst that can happen is an argument with a parks inspector. The advent of the news cable companies with their encouragement of video journalists and video paparazzi is likely to make this worse. What ought to be given some thought is the legacy of bad feelings which will remain for any return visit or approach from another production company.

One favourite west London park formerly ran a system of issuing day permits from its superintendent's office at opening time in return for a small fixed fee. Various crews began ignoring procedure and even bounced cheques. After a clampdown, unauthorised crews were escorted to the gate and anyone seeking permission would be obliged to enter into a written correspondence with the town hall.

The majority of open spaces, particularly urban ones, are administered by local government authorities. There is no common procedure for seeking filming permission and in many cases different properties in the same town might come under the Engineers Department, Highways Department or Tourist Office. It not always easy to find out which department to approach and it is not always obvious which local authority is responsible. A space like a village green might be administered by a parish or a district authority or a county or a county borough council. In recent years local authorities have been repeatedly tampered with by central government. Many historic counties have been dismembered and new counties created and then in some cases the new counties abolished in turn. Some district authorities have become all-purpose unitary authorities but others have not. London has the distinction of being the only European capital city with no overall local government at all, and two sides of a street are likely to be administered by two completely independent borough councils.

The regional film commissions are in part established to help productions, particularly foreign visiting ones, to navigate through this seemingly impenetrable muddle. The systematic privatisation, or opting out, of many local government services and the replacement of council employees by contract security companies has not helped matters. Characteristically London, which is the busiest location of all, is the last to get a commission (due in 1996).

London poses an additional set of problems. A large number of its most obvious locations are Royal Parks or Royal Palaces. As such they have their own system of policing and park rangers. They also have comprehensive sets of their own by-laws which are posted at all main gates. Some, such as a prohibition on blowing trumpets or stuffing feather mattresses in Kensington Gardens, may or not impinge upon a shooting script.

The Royal Parks are:

Bushey Park	**St James's Park**
Hyde Park	**Kensington Gardens**
Richmond Park	**Victoria Towers Gardens**
Greenwich Park	**Green Park**
Regent's Park	**Primrose Hill**

Permission to film is obtained from:

The Royal Parks Office
Rangers Lodge
Hyde Park
London W2 2UH

The Royal Palaces in the London area are:

The Tower of London	**Hampton Court**
Kensington Palace	**Banqueting House, Whitehall**
Kew Palace	

Permission to work here and certain other royal properties outside the capital can be obtained from:

The Historic Royal Palaces Agency
Apartment 38
Hampton Court Palace
East Molesley
Surrey KT8 9AU

Permission to film is not automatically given. A production is more likely to be accepted in, for example Hyde Park, if the subject is some aspect of the park itself, less likely if the intention is just to use the property as a background for a pop video. Written application is expected a minimum of one week in advance and payment must be received before shooting begins.

Ministry of Defence property

Huge areas of the UK are administered by the Ministry of Defence (MoD) including great swathes of the counties of Dorset, Wiltshire and Suffolk. Properties run by the MoD or by individual units of the armed services range from dockyards and air bases to regimental museums and Territorial Army halls. Some of these are firmly out of bounds and any attempt to play fast and loose with security regulations will result in very serious trouble indeed. Many places, however, are available for film and television, and army ranges, when not in use, are particularly attractive for staging all kinds of spectacular special effect and battle sequences. These areas are designed for smoke and loud bangs; often they have miles of road and trackway where there is no problem of disturbing or being disturbed by the public and you are unlikely to harm anyone but yourselves. Some ranges contain surprising locations such as abandoned villages. Some have become renowned wildlife refuges. Over the years repeated bombardment is apparently less harmful to the environment than recent farming practices and tourism.

If an MoD property is attractive the best plan is to seek out the relevant Commanding Officer and ask permission. In many cases the Commanding Officer will have the last word anyway and will be able to advise how high up the chain of command your request needs be taken. If you cannot get satisfactory answers locally, or want to involve more than one facility or armed service, you are advised to first contact the public relations officers for the relevant service. All reside at the same address.

For the Public Relations Officer (Army) and Public Relations Officer (Air Force) write to:

Ministry of Defence
Room 0355
Main Building
Whitehall
London SW1A 2HB

Public Relations Officer (Navy) is found at Room 0363.

For advice on gaining access to property administered by other Central Government Departments, a good start would be:

The Press Office
Department of National Heritage
Room 203
2–4 Cockspur Street
London SW1 5DH

Other institutions

The majority of institutional locations do not come under either local or national government administration, and with the progressive privatisation of public utilities fewer and fewer will do so.

First the good news

Many institutions such as schools, colleges, hospitals and even municipal graveyards are no longer guarded by impenetrable bureaucracies and can make their own decisions locally. Many places which until recently were suspicious or closed to productions now welcome them with open arms.

Now the bad news

Thanks to the enterprise culture the days are long gone when public institutions were willing to open their doors for a nominal contribution or the promise of a video cassette. Most will have their hands out for cash and many have a shrewd idea how to bargain for the best deal. More money can be squeezed out of a feature film or television commercial than a corporate video or a local documentary, but in many cases there is a bottom line minimum. In some cases institutions have banded together to rationalise fees. For example, the colleges and the University of Oxford now delegate all requests through the Bursar of Balliol College, who drives a hard bargain.

Many similar groupings have long since either imposed or advised a scale of fees for their members or associates, and in many cases have their own terms of contract, insurance requirements and waiting lists. A selection of the most important includes:

The British Library
British Museum
Great Russell Street
London WC1B 3DG

English Heritage
23 Savile Row
London W1X 1AB

The Forestry Commission
231 Corstophine Road
Edinburgh EH12 7AT

The Historic Houses Association
2 Chester Street
London SW1X 7BB

The Landmark Trust
Shottesbrooke
Maidenhead
Berkshire SL6 3SW

The Maritime Trust
2 Greenwich Church Street
Greenwich
London SE1 9BG

The National Trust
36 Queen Anne's Gate
London SW1H 9AS

Commercial property

A great number of desirable locations are wholly owned by individuals or companies and so permission to shoot should be a simple matter of direct local negotiation. But this is not always the case. Property rights are very complicated. The owner of the freehold of a property may need consultation but the occupant of a shop or house may be a tenant or sub-tenant who also needs to give consent. Agricultural property raises complex questions of landowners and tenants. Often both freehold and leasehold are complicated by the rights of third parties who have rights of way and access. There may be insurance implications if permission is granted by a party not properly authorised to do so.

Permission to shoot in a market or a shopping mall does not include permission to shoot at any particular premises, in fact many shopkeepers will object to you shooting their window displays though as often as not this is because of a crew blocking an entrance and driving away customers.

Many markets are tightly regulated and the market inspectors have waiting lists to control the numbers of visiting crews and impose a scale of fees. The inspectors should always be located before any market scenes are begun. Most urban shopping centres are dominated by stores belonging to major chains, many of which are very concerned about their public images. Getting permission to shoot in these often involves lengthy correspondence with highly suspicious press or public relations officers. Even small enterprises may show reluctance to cooperate particularly if this is not the first visit of a location crew. The reasons are fairly clear.

- Customers are reluctant to enter a shop where a television crew is working. Lights, cables and tripods block windows and counters. Staff posing for cameras are not serving customers and customers watching a performance are not buying goods.
- A conscientious recordist will always ask for background music or public address systems to be switched off and may complain about the sound of air conditioning.
- When lighting is involved the electrician will very likely start tampering with the mains power supply and complaining about the problems of mixed fluorescent, tungsten and daylight.
- Too often directors appear to become monsters demanding silence, ordering staff and clients to repeat actions and stopping people going about their business or from getting into shots.

For every member of the public who would go to the stake for the opportunity to be seen on television there are two who would run a mile to avoid it. The quickest way to empty a hotel lounge or a betting shop is to turn up with a camera. A surprising number of people are not where or with whom they are supposed to be. Hotels are very sensitive. They might let you shoot in their cocktail bar, but you will have to provide your own extras. A bucolic scene of rural cider making can lead to the whole workforce taking to the hills at the cry of 'Action' if they happen to be drawing unemployment or social security payments at the time.

The answer, if time and money allow, is to wait until after hours to do the filming. This will allow optimum control over sound and lighting. If the project is any kind of drama or dramatised documentary this will be the only way to work.

There is unfortunately the problem of extra payments for staff and facilities. Caretakers, security guards and local electricians may have to be retained after their normal working hours. They have no obligation to agree to do so and will anyhow have to be paid their normal overtime rates. It may be difficult to arrange for such facilities as car parking or lavatories to be kept open. Automatic security systems may have to be disabled and the police informed. If there is a local telephone exchange, there may have to be arrangements made for the routing of calls. If members of the staff or public are needed at awkward times, problems arise over taxis, catering and even babysitters.

None of these problems is insurmountable so long as the director comes clean about the implications of the shoot. Outsiders rarely comprehend how slow and drawn out shooting can be. Inexperienced directors are frequently wildly optimistic about how many shots they can get in the can during a day. The important thing is to be absolutely clear what you intend and come clean about the time and staff implications, as well as whether it is going to be necessary to dress sets and move existing fixtures and fittings.

Productions that attempt to deceive location owners about their requirements will not be allowed back at best but at worst may be asked to stop shooting before they have finished or have permission for the use of the footage withheld.

Private houses

Everything said about commercial premises applies to the use of private houses. The occupants of historic houses are often members of associations which advise on fees and conditions for television crews. There are picturesque villages and historic streets where the householders have come to regard visiting crews as a regular supplementary source of income. Ordinary householders may be flattered to receive a visit from a team from a television station. But again too many enthusiastic directors have behaved like Atilla the Hun when dealing with Joe Public.

In all honesty a visiting crew is likely to rearrange the furniture, tamper with the electrics, borrow the telephone, fill the sink with coffee cups, eat the last chocolate biscuit, give the cat a nervous breakdown and spark off a neighbourhood war by blocking drives and occupying parking spaces.

Be honest. Offer some small facility fee even if only to cover the refreshments and electricity. Most people will forgive the muddy boots on the carpet in return for a VHS copy of the production. If a fee or tape is offered, make sure it actually arrives. Directors who make promises they have no intention of keeping leave behind a surprising amount of bitterness.

A word of warning
If it is intended to shoot over a period of days, be careful about continuity and the over-enthusiastic resident. One production was completely thrown when the occupants of a particularly squalid squat were smitten by house pride and re-papered the wall in between shoots.

Theatres and concert halls

These are appealing locations but can raise their own very particular problems.

Lighting

Most halls have some kind of provision for stage lighting. At the village hall or scout hut end of the market, the electrics can be of a very dubious quality. They have to be checked by a qualified electrician before any additional lighting is installed. The solution of putting a nail in the fuse box to allow it to cope temporarily has fairly obvious health, safety and insurance implications.

More professional set-ups will have their own electricians and, if a production is in performance, their own lighting designer. The television and stage electricians will have to agree a working arrangement and union regulations may come into play. The television director and cameraman will have to decide whether existing stage lighting will be suitable as it is, whether to negotiate resetting any of the lamps or to introduce additional ones.

Safety

Theatres are governed by very strict safety and licensing arrangements. Above all camera crews will not be permitted to block any fire lanes or exits either front of house or backstage. So no camera will be allowed, for example, in a centre aisle during a performance. The only solution if often to place a camera in the middle of the auditorium with the result that a number of seats must be reserved, both those occupied by camera and crew and those behind whose sightlines will be blocked. The television production will be expected to pay for these in addition to any other agreed fees. In the event of several crews being involved or an outside broadcast envisaged the local fire officer may have to be consulted.

Union agreements

Under no circumstances should a director get involved in trying to mix amateur and professional performers and technicians. The demarcation line between professional and amateur status is jealously guarded (see Chapter 6). There are complex agreements involving British Actors' Equity, the Musicians' Union and BECTU, which complicate the shooting of any performance either in rehearsal or on stage.

Briefly a television production may only shoot limited undirected documentary footage of professional performers without incurring a complete set of performance fees and contractual conditions. This applies even to military bands, many of which belong *en masse* to the Musicians' Union. Any interference by the television director – even as small as a request for an actor to move out of a camera shot or a band to repeat a particular tune – constitutes direction and thereby attracts a fee. The fees depend on context but are agreed and fixed. All possible Union agreement problems must be sorted out before anything further can be arranged and even then technicians or artists who have not received individual approaches are quite capable of refusing to cooperate on the day for no apparent reason. Preferably initial approaches should be made to locally elected union officials, but if problems arise or details of national agreements have to be verified the organisations responsible are:

 British Actors' Equity Association
Guild House
Upper St Martin's Lane
London WC2H 9EG

The Musicians' Union (MU)
60–62 Clapham Road
London SW9 0JJ

Broadcasting, Entertainment, Cinematograph and Theatre Union (BECTU)
111 Wardour Street
London W1Y 4AY

The great outdoors

Wide open spaces appear to be free from complication. Again it ain't necessarily so. All land is owned by someone even so-called common land and national parks. In practice it is not possible to check out ownership and filming permission for every little set-up in the countryside but as usual the more ambitious the production the greater the risk of becoming a trespasser.

Contrary to common opinion there is no general law of trespass in England. (Scottish law has no provision for trespass at all but it also does not recognise freehold land tenure.)

The familiar sign 'Trespassers will be prosecuted' is what lawyers dryly call a wooden falsehood. Such a notice expresses the owner's wishes but has no backing in criminal law. A landowner can, however, try to prevent trespass and remove trespassers by using reasonable force. Reasonable force is defined as the minimum required to oblige the trespasser to leave and the amount of resistance offered. In effect the landowner risks committing the more serious offence of assault, which does not require physical harm to occur. Threatening a trespasser with physical violence can constitute assault, particularly if a weapon is involved. A landowner can seek redress for trespass only if there is injury to his or her person, land or goods. Trampled crops, broken hedges, gates left open and dogs allowed free amongst livestock are common examples.

No production wants to be ordered off the land by an angry owner or confronted by a farmer for straying from public rights of way. The easiest preventative measure is always to carry a large-scale Ordnance Survey map of each district and to keep to the system of footpaths and bridle ways. The Public Order Act has now created a new criminal offence of aggravated trespass. The new law is intended to enable the police to act against large numbers of squatters, protest demonstrators occupying property, and organisers of unauthorised 'rave' parties or gatherings of New Age travellers on private property. Presumably the law could be invoked against a film or television production. As things have stood in the past, the police have been very reluctant to get involved in disputes about trespass.

Finding locations

For most factual programmes the choice of location is limited by the subject but anything involving dramatisation or demonstration may require a search for somewhere both suitable and affordable. A good starting point is the biggest local estate agents. There are often a number of vacant residential and commercial properties available for filming in return for a payment and the usual indemnities. For really large unoccupied spaces you might contact:

The National Association of Warehouse Keepers
418–422 Strand
London WC2R 0PT

> *A point to remember*
> Many vacant properties have their gas, water telephone and electricity disconnected. Reconnection may be essential for technical production reasons, or hygiene and health and safety concerns. The relevant utilities companies must be notified in advance and will expect reconnection/disconnection charges to be paid.

There are a multitude of official organisations and associations dealing with everything from churches and chapels to playing fields and lighthouses. An excellent listing of many of these will be found in *The Television Researcher's Guide* by Kathy Chater, published by BBC Television Training, BBC Elstree Centre, Borehamwood, Herts.

There are a number of commercial location finders regularly advertised in the trade press and in reference directories who keep their own indexes of available locations and will have instant information about available properties and scales of fees.

A particularly important advance has been the setting up by the British Film Commission of FIND, the Film Information National Database, which networks information from the national and the regional film commissions and hopes to expand into an almost comprehensive national directory of suitable locations defined as follows:

A location can be any type of place or landscape and those held by FIND are wide-ranging with details of castles, stately homes, public buildings, farms, run-down tenement blocks, terraces of Victorian houses, airports, factories, lighthouses, schools, churches, and much more all available for filming. Landscapes with special features such as bridges, mazes, boat-houses, streams etc., are equally important.

This computerised library of locations is added to and revised on a daily basis. FIND is accessed through:

The British Film Commission
70 Baker Street
London W1M 1DJ

Note that the function of the Commission is to promote the UK as an attractive location for overseas film productions to which it offers (for free) a whole range of production services which are also listed in FIND.

For domestic productions it is more appropriate to approach one of the regional film commissions whose services to producers are also free and whose brief is to attract production to their particular areas.

It is hoped that before long every city and region will be covered by a film commission.

At the time of writing there are sixteen in operation with a seventeenth for London at last projected for 1996. Addresses for those already in existence are as follows:

Bath Film Office
Abbey Chambers
Abbey Church Yard
Bath BA1 1LY

Cardiff Film Commission
North Chambers
Castle Arcade
Cardiff CF1 2BX

Central England Screen Commission
Waterside House
46 Gas Street
Birmingham B1 2JT

Eastern Screen
Anglia Television
Prince of Wales Road
Norwich NR1 3JG

Edinburgh and Lothian Screen Industries Office
Filmhouse
88 Lothian Road
Edinburgh EH3 9BZ

Gwynedd Film Office
Gwynedd County Council
Economic Development and Planning Department
Llys-y-Bont
Parc Menai
Bangor
Gwynedd LL57 4BN

Highland Regional Council
Regional Buildings
Glenurquart Road
Inverness IV 5NX

Isle of Man Commission
Sea Terminal
Douglas
Isle of Man

Liverpool Film Office
Central Libraries
William Brown Street
Liverpool L3 8EW

London Film Commission (from late 1996)
Carnival Film
12 Raddington Road
Ladbroke Grove
London W10 5TG

Northern Screen Commission
Stonehills
Shields Road
Gateshead NE10 0HW

Scottish Screen Locations
Filmhouse
88 Lothian Road
Edinburgh EH3 9BZ

Screen Wales
Canolfan Sgrin Centre
Llandaff
Cardiff CF5 2PU

South West Film Commission
18 Belle View Road
Saltash
Cornwall PL12 6TG

South West Scotland Film Commission
Gracefield Arts Centre
28 Edinburgh Road
Dumfries DG1 1JQ

Yorkshire Screen Commission
Unit 416
The Workstation
15 Paternoster Road
Sheffield S1 2BX

In addition some local government authorities have set up their own commissions, such as the Ealing Film Office. Services range from providing municipal dustcarts to constructing special road signs to order. Contact:

Press Office
First Floor, Perceval House
14–16 Uxbridge Road
Ealing, London W5 2HL

Location contracts

It follows from all that has been said above that the relationship between a production team and a location owner can be extremely fraught and the possibilities for misunderstanding are legion. Because no two productions will make the same demands on a location and no two location owners will have the same anticipation about fees, the British and the regional film offices will not get involved in the negotiation of payments. But whether the production entails a simple interview in a council house or a re-enactment of the Battle of Stalingrad the first priority is *get it in writing.*

Large national broadcasters have a printed document known as a Facility Form which is used for all simple shoots. PACT has drawn up a model location agreement letter which is available to all members.

Note

The finest location database of all has been built up by the BBC. It contains many thousands of locations, from stately homes to swimming pools, with over ten thousand photographs. Currently it is only open to BBC productions and those directly commissioned by the BBC, but some limited location advice service may become available in the future.

The reason for this exclusivity are worth noting by anyone thinking of setting up their own modest location database, and a good reminder of the pitfalls in wait for programme makers beneath the simplest matters.

These days almost any such records will be scanned into a computer database, and as such they are subject to the Data Protection Act. Details of properties are covered as much as details of the owners, who have the right to know and amend the contents.

Photographs raise issues of copyright, particularly those taken from magazine articles, press cuttings or stills of previous productions.

Some owners prefer to negotiate an exclusive private contract with one known and trusted company, and do not want a procession of researchers beating a path to their door.

Most important of all, any good recce by a researcher or location manager will note details such as ease of rear access, working hours of staff, valuable fixtures, location of main utilities and possibly sketch plans of rooms and grounds, with details of spare sets of keys. The information needed to ensure a smooth location shoot is also a perfect blueprint for burglary. The programme maker has an obligation of confidentiality.

In both cases the simple letter, often signed on the spot, states:

- That the owner gives authorisation to film interiors and exteriors as defined and bring such personnel and equipment as may be required. The person giving authorisation also warrants that he or she has the right to do so.
- Which dates and times are agreed.
- That the property owner assigns all rights to the filming and

assigns all rights for the exploitation of the material to the production.

- That the production indemnifies the owner against any damage caused by negligence.
- What fee is agreed, together with VAT, and how calculated e.g. by day or half day.

Note that the facility/location agreement form is only about the rights to use property. If the intention is also to interview any of the occupants they ought to be paid a separate fee and sign an interview release form, known informally in the BBC as a 'blood chit'. This need be no more than a short two-paragraph note saying:

- The interviewee agrees to accept the fee offered.
- The interviewee agrees to assign all rights in the filming to the production company.
- The interviewee agrees that the interview may be edited and that there is no obligation on behalf of the production to use all or any of it in the final programme.

Model contracts for independent producers are issued by:

PACT
Gordon House
Greencoat Place
London SW1P 1PH

PACT Scotland
Dowanhill
74 Victoria Crescent Road
Glasgow G12 9JN

Since 1995 there has been an independent organisation jointly serving PACT members and the ITV broadcast companies. For information contact:

The Producers' Industrial Relations Service
15 Berners Street
London W1P 3DE

Model agreements are all very well but there will always be location owners who want to query the small print and may object to assigning all rights, or may agree to filming but not agree to publicity stills, or may insist that the property is or is not properly named and identified on screen. The canny location owner faced with the demands of a feature film or television drama will want to negotiate a very detailed contract. Any variety of exclusions and restrictions may be requested by either an owner or the insurers

21

of the property. Again PACT can help with suggested outline legal agreements.

The film commissions have to be even handed in these matters. They want to attract as many productions as possible to their respective patches. But they have to keep the owners of locations happy both for local goodwill and, of course, funding and the need to keep good locations on the books. A location lost through disagreement or bad behaviour is not likely to be regained easily.

The South West Film Commission has drawn up a set of guidelines for the owners of private property which essentially are questions which ought to be answered before consent is given. Producers and directors are advised to have ready answers to each of them before setting off on the road.

- Is the production company *bona fide* and recognised?
- How does the company intend to use the building and are there any special effects involved?
- What are the intended hours or days including setting up and clearing up afterwards?
- Which interiors and exteriors are required, including those for access or for lighting, and are there any off-limit areas?
- Will there be any alterations made to the property and what will be done about re-instatement?
- What are the numbers of crew, artists, extras or support services envisaged?
- Are there any special arrangements for security whilst the crew is on site?
- Will any of the owner's furniture be required and if so what measures will be taken to protect it and fittings such as carpets?
- If any of the owner's property has to be removed how will it be stored and what arrangements have been made for insurance?
- What does the production intend to bring on to the property as dressing and action props, or even animals?
- How many crew vehicles are there, where will they park, what access will they need? Where will the owner or the neighbours or visitors park in the meantime?
- What catering arrangements will be requested and what will be provided?
- What are the requirements for washrooms and lavatories?
- What is going to done about payment for water and electricity and the disposal of waste?

- Will the crew need storage space or will the performers need make-up and costume areas?
- Does the owner have any house rules such as no smoking, or no food or drink on set?
- Will the occupants be required to vacate the property for any period and if so what recompense will be offered for alternative accommodation and eating and travel expenses?
- Who is responsible for clearing up after the shoot and what are the arrangements for restoring any damage?
- What is the contract being offered and how is it calculated?
- Will the production company give its own insurance details and if requested provide an insurance cover note for the intended period of filming? The owner's insurance company will ask to be notified and they may need confirmation of the arrangements if existing insurance is not to be invalidated or an additional premium required.

In a simple form all these questions are as applicable to a half- day shoot in somebody's shop or office as to the requisitioning of a stately home for a costume drama. Even if you have signed only the most simple facility form, the director must be prepared for the eventualities. Furniture and curtains should be rearranged as they were before the shoot. Bathrooms and kitchens should be cleaned up. Recompense should be offered for food consumed or looted during the day and for telephone calls made from the premises. In the case of large properties a cash tip to a janitor, caretaker or groundsman can ensure that things are set right but agreement should be made in advance. Do not allow crews to smoke or drop food on the carpets. Respect lawns and gardens particularly. A bunch of weeds to the driver or electrician is somebody else's prize specimen.

Should things go horribly wrong, behave as advised in traffic accidents.

- Do not make a panic personal offer of compensation as this is an immediate admission of guilt.
- Note down all the circumstances immediately.
- Verify the insurance details of both parties.
- Notify the production company insurers as soon as possible.

However, if the incident involves harm to individuals and the producer is shown to be guilty of neglecting health and safety regulations then not only may the insurance be invalidated but criminal prosecution by the Health and Safety Executive as well as a civil case for damages many follow (see Chapter 13).

In the past fixing locations was done directly by the producer, director or researcher with the support of a PA. In large productions a great deal would be handled by the production manager.

In the current state of accountancy-dominated television, directors or reporters sally forth with two- or even one-man crews and the PA is in many companies becoming an endangered species reduced to office duties. Broadcast companies have enthusiastically reduced or sold off many of their programme support services. Independent producers can rarely afford long-term staff. So it may be advantageous for a production to hire in a production manager or a location manager for the required period particularly if the producer and director concerned are themselves too pressed for time or unsure about handling the logistics of locations (this book ought to help). A really ambitious production might need both a production manager and a locations manager.

Both crafts have set up associations and registers of members:

The Guild of Location Managers
14 Montpelier Row
Twickenham
Middlesex TW1 2NQ

The Production Managers' Association
c/o PACT
10 Greencoat Place
London SW1P 1PH

2
FOREIGN AFFAIRS

Working on overseas locations has tremendous appeal. The opportunities for foreign travel at somebody else's expense is one of the great attractions of a career in television.

After facing the realities of shooting in exotic places though, many producers and directors decide that foreign travel is something they can happily do without. There is an ocean of difference between setting out on holiday with a case of amateur equipment and trying to cart a small mountain of flight cases around the world in an endless cycle of bureaucratic obstruction and non-cooperation of airport staff. Bright-eyed enthusiasm from the new director may not be reciprocated by an experienced production team who have had their fill of the interiors of aircraft and hotel bedrooms and know only too well the consequences of drinking the local water.

Even well-reconnoitred locations can suffer from unexpected spanners thrown into the works by officialdom, suddenly non-cooperative local associates, political events, illness and the weather.

Film and television crews are internationally reputed to be extravagantly wealthy so that the budget can look like a honey pot to every rapacious hotelier, guide, taxi driver and local official. Local standards of punctuality and trustworthiness may be very different from those expected from professionals at home. Some people have the right temperament for working abroad and some definitely do not, which is something to keep in mind when picking a crew for foreign adventures.

Getting there

By land

If the proposed locations are in member countries of the European Union (EU), it may be economical for the team to travel by their own transport. This avoids all the problems of airports and local vehicle hire. Many cameramen have their own specially customised and equipped cars or vans which they much prefer to travel in. All the producer needs to agree is the fee for the use of the vehicle and calculate the fuel, insurance, ferry and toll implications. However, if overland transport is chosen note the following points:

- A cameraman may be willing to carry an assistant or recordist in the vehicle but may be much less enthusiastic about acting as the unit bus service. The larger the unit the greater the number of vehicles involved. Similarly members of the unit may not be at all happy about being crammed into a van for hours on end just to save costs. Hiring a car or minibus locally might still work out less troublesome.

- A laden vehicle may be subject to speed restrictions and there may be company or union restrictions on the number of hours a driver may be expected to be at the wheel and regulations about rest and meal breaks. Crossing the channel does not mean waving farewell to British health and safety regulations as most are in line with European laws anyway. In some instances, problems may be more complicated. For example continental drivers of vehicles greater than five tons may only drive between certain hours and not at all during prescribed lunch breaks or on weekends or public holidays. Travel times should always be calculated very generously and consideration given to rest and meal times as well as recovery and unpacking times on arrival.

- If non-EU countries are included in the itinerary then driving licence and vehicle document requirements as well as insurance implications must be checked. Crossing land frontiers, particularly when carrying quantities of equipment, might raise more problems than arrival at an international airport.

Hiring vehicles

The hire of vehicles needs careful costing. Self-drive cars are simply arranged and reasonably cheap in the UK, so much so that it is always worth considering whether to hire cars even for low budget productions at home rather than face the mileage and insurance problems of unit members using their own transport. However, in some countries this may not be the case.

The major international car hire firms will often be able to quote a price for vehicles at foreign affiliates but in many cases this works out more expensive than cars hired on the spot. The advantage is that any disputes can be pursued through a British head office. Even with the largest international companies, local insurance provisions and hire conditions may vary considerably. For example, collision insurance waivers may be hedged in with provisos and in Central America the insured may be held totally responsible in the event of theft. Cars hired in Greece may not be insured against damage to tyres or the undersides of vehicles.

The mechanical condition of cars provided even by the largest companies is sometimes lamentable. So if hiring location transport abroad check:

- Have all the proposed drivers got appropriate driving licences? The current EU-style British driving licences are valid in most parts of the world but some countries demand licences with photographs. Such licences are currently proposed for the UK but their introduction is opposed by some civil liberties groups. Appropriate international driving licences are obtainable from local offices of the Automobile Association or the Royal Automobile Club. Some countries such as the Peoples' Republic of China either do not allow self-drive vehicles or restrict their use. Women are not allowed to drive in some Islamic countries and may be ill advised to do so in others.

- What are the precise insurance limitations for vehicle damage and also drivers and third parties? Even in some European countries a driver may be detained by the police for lengthy periods in the event of an accident regardless of culpability. In the USA third-party cover of as little as $25,000 is available, but for so notoriously litigious a country, cover of a million dollars at least is advisable, and is offered as an option by reputable hire firms. Drink-driving laws are often draconian. In several European countries and some of the states of the USA insurance is completely invalidated if the driver has any drop of alcohol in the bloodstream.

- Is the available transport going to be adequate or appropriate for the needs of the production? Even if the main unit fits into a minibus there are likely to be occasions when more than one vehicle will be essential. It has been commented that the one kind of car which is equally at home on motorways, mountain tracks, mud and moor land is a hire car. None the less in some countries the expense of a four-wheel drive vehicle might prove a good investment. In this case it would be an advantage for at least one driver to have some idea of all-terrain driving and knowledge of basic maintenance. There are surprising numbers of British drivers who have no idea how to change a wheel.

Hiring drivers

The solution, sometimes not a costly one, is to arrange for local drivers as well as vehicles. The obvious advantages are:

- Language problems cease to be a problem, except those

between the crew and the hired driver.

- The local driver will be familiar with local traffic conventions and know the approved etiquette when confronted by traffic police, parking regulations, road blocks or bullock carts.
- In theory navigation should be easy. In practice local drivers in some countries have an uncanny ability to get lost and a total inability to read a road map.
- In the event of an accident it will be the driver who is arrested (or in some cases lynched by the locals); for breakdowns the driver can negotiate replacement cars, spare parts and repairs.
- Locating a mechanically safe and insured vehicle driven by a reliable chauffeur who can understand adequate English is not always easy. Usually this is left to the fixer (see below) who not infrequently is personally involved in the car or taxi rental business.

An option frequently overlooked is the national and local tourist offices. These can be invaluable in cutting through red tape and can arrange suitable cars at a fixed daily rate driven by chauffeurs used to foreigners. However, it must be confirmed at the outset whether such drivers are available to work irregular hours or on weekends or holidays. An overseas shoot is hostage to its transport.

Be very cautious when privately negotiating local transport hire or agreeing that locally hired personnel use their own transport. Those involved may have their own ideas about calculating fuel costs, mileage charges, travel times and hours of availability. Additional gratuities may be expected as a matter of course for anything not clearly specified. If you have to promise these, try to hold back payment until everyone has been safely delivered to the airport departure gate.

By air

Air travel is by far the easiest and often the only way to reach a foreign location but can still raise problems for both crews and equipment. If the production is not going to start in tears, let alone end in them, certain preliminary precautions are needed:

- tickets;
- visas;
- inoculations;
- rendezvous times and local transport.

Any production will try to arrange the cheapest deals available for airline tickets, from normal APEX fares to special bucket shop deals, charter flights and flying by obscure airlines. Almost all cheap deals involve lengthy advanced non-refundable booking and no flexibility in the dates of return. If the production is going to cut costs and book tickets for the whole unit, or allow a client or sponsor to fix flights, a few points must be noted:

- Is everyone agreed about travelling together both ways?
- Working abroad is no holiday at the best of times but a private holiday after the end of a shoot is often the great incentive for joining an overseas production. In which case flexible, refundable or open-return tickets will be needed.
- Cheap deals can be a false economy if for any reason additional shooting days are needed, or members of the production team are called on to stay on for additional research or to solve local problems; or for that matter an unanticipated change in the politics or the climate or health problems requires some or all of the unit to leave early.
- Cheap deals usually involve travelling by the cheapest available class which inevitably results in seating designed for midgets and poor to dreadful food. What is acceptable, just, for a brief flight to a European capital might be intolerable for a flight to the Far East or South America.
- Cheap passenger deals might not involve savings on excess baggage (see below) and under some circumstances it can be better for the efficiency of the production and possibly financially advantageous to think about upgrading tickets to club or even first class so as to use the pooled baggage allowances of the team.

Airline companies which offer the cheapest deals often do so for the good reason that passengers are hard to find. PACT recommends that productions only travel with airlines belonging to IATA (the International Air Traffic Association). Although a strict adherence to this advice would rule out some of the excellent Far Eastern airlines, it might help avoid unhappy involvement with the sort of companies whose in-flight catering is restricted to dubious sandwiches and whose planes are impounded before take-off for non-payment of fuel bills.

All long-distance air travel is stressful and travelling as part of a location unit is more stressful of all. There has to be time allocated for crews and performers to recuperate and, if necessary, recover from jet lag. As a guideline PACT suggests that for any trip involving more than four hours' flight time there should be a scheduled rest period of not less than ten hours after arrival at the final destination and a rest of 24 hours should be allowed for any trip involving a flight time of ten hours or more. If the flights have crossed a large number of time zones, such as between Europe and the Far East, or if tourist class seating prevented sleep en route, these allowances may be inadequate.

Inoculations

Airlines travelling to or between tropical destinations may refuse to carry passengers without the relevant certificates of inoculation, particularly between regions prone to epidemics or where yellow fever is endemic. It is a sensible precaution to require all crew members travelling to the tropics to have a complete set of inoculations before departure and as some of these for first-time travellers have to be staggered over a period of weeks it is as well to make this clear as early as possible. Some countries have very specific requirements. Saudi Arabia may require a certificate of freedom from AIDS for those working there for more than a short visit. For the most up to date health information supplied by the World Health Authority and the London School of Hygiene and Tropical Medicine, enquiries should be addressed to the nearest MASTA clinic.

Travelling abroad always involves some health risk which increases the further you work from the sanitised environs of tourist hotels.

Some minor problems variously called 'Bombay Belly', 'Gippy Tummy' and 'The Aztec Two Step' are probably unavoidable and the best medical advice is to let them run their course and accept that the sufferers may be incapacitated for a day or two.

Of greater concern are water-borne diseases like cholera, typhoid and amoebic dysentery which can be avoided by simple hygiene and by making sure that the unit is well supplied with bottled beer or water, washes fruit, avoids salads and ice cubes, and so on.

The disease giving the greatest concern at present is malaria, which has been making a reappearance even around the Mediterranean and is almost universal in areas of sub-Saharan Africa. New strains of the disease are regularly evolving so that there are areas where not one but two or more sets of prophylactic pills are prescribed. Although in most cases malaria resembles a severe case of 'flu, there are cerebral strains which kill.

The commonest danger in many developing country comes not from disease but from traffic accidents, which can be hideously apparent during the taxi drive from the airport to the hotel. It is important therefore that everyone is aware of their blood group and that this is known to the production leader.

Health tip

Because of the rapidly changing profile of diseases, the London School of Tropical Medicine and Hygiene together with British Airways have established the Medical Advisory Service For Travellers Abroad (MASTA).

MASTA offers a 24-hour health brief for travellers based on the latest advice of the World Health Authority and the Foreign Office.

MASTA also has clinics in most large cities and all major British airports which will dispense the relevant injections and pills as well as supply equipment such as mosquito nets, water-purifying equipment and insect repellents.

The risk of contracting AIDS or hepatitis B and C means that it is important for the production unit to take prepared AIDS packs containing sterile hypodermics, surgical needles, etc.

 MASTA
Keppel Street
London WC 1E 7HT
Tel. 0891 224 100

The insurance implications of overseas working are mentioned below (p. 95).

Visas

Many countries demand visas and as airlines are held responsible for the repatriation of passengers denied entry, they will not carry passengers without the correct documents. Visa requirements are often the result of a complicated diplomatic game of tit-for-tat and can come and go according to the vagaries of international politics. The lack of a visa requirement generally denotes the existence of a bilateral agreement between governments.

Many visas are just a formality and are issued at the port of entry, sometimes free or sometimes for a fee. But often visas have to be applied for at the consulate or embassy which in turn frequently refer applications to their own foreign offices for approval. This can result in delays of days or even months. Journalists and television crews are often regarded with particular suspicion and some countries seem to enjoy playing a hair-raising game of brinkmanship by not returning passports until the very eve of departure.

Travel agents will sometimes undertake to get the commonest visas but for many parts of the world only personal applications will work unless visitors are members of an approved group tour.

Care should be taken that earlier passport stamps or visas do not upset sensitivities. For many years the existence of a South African entry stamp would bar the bearer from most African countries and only a couple of Islamic countries will allow entry to any passport holder who has evidently visited Israel. As a last resort application might have to be made to the passport office for a new document. Many countries will not issue visas to passports with less than six months validity to run.

The exact passport status of every member of a travelling unit has to be checked. There are different status British passports for full British citizens and overseas British passports granted to those born in colonies or Commonwealth countries. A Republic of Ireland passport has long been regarded as a great asset for news crews since Ireland has shown very limited potential for upsetting other governments but is very often diplomatically represented at British embassies none the less. On occasions like the Falklands conflict the carriers of Irish passports had a happy freedom to travel in South America. But mysteriously some Central American states demand visas for the Irish although not British passport holders.

During the dispute over nuclear testing in the South Pacific, New Zealand and French passport holders have had a particularly hard time from each others' immigration departments.

Passport tip
There are several London-based commercial agencies which will both advise on obtaining visas and subsequently do the necessary leg-work around the embassies. For productions with personnel based outside the capital these services may be a particularly good investment. One such agency with experience of television crews is:

The Visa and Passport Service
St Stephens Mews
London W2 5QZ

They have a bureau at the Passport Office and will also undertake to obtain replacement and second passports.

Rendezvous times and transport

Travelling with a production unit is not as simple as travelling as an individual. It is sometimes essential for all the personnel to meet before embarking on the formalities at the airport and if collective baggage allowances are to be used, everyone must obviously be together. Checking in several hours in advance is almost always essential for both security clearances and going through the paperwork formalities for any equipment. The airline personnel or your shipping agent should advise on the required time-scale as well as local details like the times customs staff are available. Even if unit members are expected to make their own way to the airport of departure it is essential to have made firm arrangements for portering and transport to hotels at the other end and ideally a fixer or official representative waiting. The morale of more than one unit has plummeted on arrival at a far-flung airport to find it either deserted or an unfathomable mad house. It is not propitious to start a trip locked in mortal combat with the native porters and taxi drivers or else sitting on a mountain of luggage watching the dawn break over a closed coffee bar.

Equipment

The availability of lightweight news cameras and the general scaling down of crew sizes, as well as technological improvements, means that it may be possible for a small unit to travel with a very small amount of equipment. Even so it is unlikely that excess baggage can be avoided entirely, particularly if the proposed shoot is for anything more than a few days' duration, or if lighting and a good supply of batteries are required. The possibilities of doing deals with airlines or of pooling personal baggage allowances has been mentioned. But excess baggage can be very expensive, even ruinously so. A pessimistic, but not unreasonable, rule of thumb for camera, sound, lighting, stock, cables and batteries for a three-man camera crew would be one and a half times the cost of a first-class ticket.

Cost is only part of the problem a production faces. The perennial nightmare is the attendant paperwork.

Technical equipment as well as costumes, make-up, scenery and props attract a wide range of import duties, purchase taxes, value-added taxes and even in some cases absolute prohibitions. To avoid unending bureaucratic delays, financial penalties or, at the very worst, the impounding of equipment most countries insist on a system of ATA (Admission Temporaire) carnets. A carnet is a sort of passport for equipment which can be issued by the chamber of commerce for the district in which the production company is based. A carnet can be applied for directly or arranged by a shipping agent, a route which is easier but more costly.

Drawing up carnets requires a large fee as well as a week or more notice. The carnet lists in the greatest detail every item of technical equipment together with estimated value and all the serial numbers. Once prepared a carnet cannot be modified so a perennial nightmare is for a camera to be found faulty on the eve of departure and an incorrectly listed substitute packed.

Apart from the fee for preparing the documentation, the production will also have to put down a security to the estimated value of the equipment and this security may be forfeit if equipment imported into a country is not shown to have left it or if equipment taken from the UK does not return. The deposit should take the form of a guaranteed bank deposit or an insurance agreement.

Although it is a fearsome sized document with multiple copies, a carnet will only remain valid for one year. Within this period, it may be used for any number of visits, always assuming that the identical equipment is taken each time. So not only is the production in hock for the value of all its gear but once a carnet is used the paperwork must be meticulously observed. Starting with the British port of departure, every time the unit arrives at or departs from a country the carnet details have to be observed and the document stamped appropriately. Not only is this a time-consuming procedure but there can be additional complications, for example the relevant customs officials may not be available at the time of departure. It is politic to give good notice in advance that carnet clearance is going to be required (this also applies to British airports for very early or late departures). At land frontiers or minor airports, officials may not request or recognise what a carnet is, in which case the temptation just to depart quietly has to be resisted. This is just asking for trouble at the next frontier or on arrival home.

Customs officials, including some of our own, will decide to check the veracity of the documentation by asking to see items of equipment. Sod's Law dictates that the item they request either:

- is at the bottom of the heaviest flight case in the pile;
- has an incorrectly typed serial number;
- is a minor item which someone has dropped over the side of a canoe.

Most customs officials will have no idea what they are looking at and so items such as batteries, cables, tape stock, maintenance tool kits and minor spares which have no manufacturer's serial identification can lead to endless multi-lingual arguments. At this point the value of having a good shipping agent and a good fixer can become apparent.

Up to 30 countries demand an ATA carnet and it is an advisable document to have for many more, but as regulations can change overnight, it is essential to contact the commercial sections of the relevant embassies before setting out. The EU has abolished its own internal carnet system and this also affects those states which have applications to join pending. At the time of writing the only West European state which still requires carnets is Norway. A few countries such as Taiwan insist on their own carnet systems.

Fortunately a lot of countries will be satisfied with a simplified list procedure. For this the production company draws up its own schedule of equipment which is copied onto multiple lists. The lists are distributed to whichever bodies may be interested on arrival and baggage can be checked against these on departure to make sure that nothing has been sold locally in the meantime. Try to get as many official stamps as possible at each time. Beware that some countries may request copies of the list in translation and others will not accept photocopies.

Even though lists are simpler and incomparably cheaper than proper carnets a visiting crew might still get a demand for a bond or bank guarantee against re-export of equipment. If this is the case it will be important to try to get the local television company, tourist board or local sponsor to stand surety. There is a logic to this. In many countries the tax on camera and electronic equipment will be greater than the original purchase price in the UK. If there is no local backing the only solution might be to arrange a customs bond with an international bank which will be in place on arrival and will be released on departure and re-export of the goods. If even this does not work, the production might have to put up its own money in the form of temporary customs duty, which is refundable on departure, and an import tax, which is not.

The complications which arise when someone loses a tripod over a cliff or the microphones get stolen are too painful to relate.

Lists may also pose problems in the UK. On departure the producer should give two copies to Customs and Excise and make sure that these are stamped, together with one for retention. On return the two lists can be compared and numbers checked as with the carnet. The concern of British customs is not so much that you may have sold your equipment on an exotic black market but that you may have replaced equipment or added to it whilst away. British customs officials can be as awkward at wanting to go through the cases as any foreign official. And, sad to relate, in the past flight cases have been used as excellent places to conceal narcotics.

Other prohibitions

Not only customs requirements create problems. The International Air Traffic Association which represents most major airlines have their own common set of restrictions. Items which may be restricted or banned include all sorts of weapons (whether fake or real), aerosols, pyrotechnics, alcohol or alcohol-based substances (an additional source of trouble at Islamic customs) medicines and animal products.

For security reasons any electronic equipment travelling as either hold or hand luggage is regarded with particular suspicion and a crew has to arrive with sufficient hours to spare to enable all the possible checks. There is a unceasing debate about whether security X-rays can damage either tape and film stock or the microchips in electronic cameras. Airports maintain that their security measures are harmless. Many operators though insist on carrying their cameras as cabin luggage and refuse to put them through the normal X-ray checks.

Hiring locally

There is always the possibility of hiring either a camera crew or equipment on arrival. If equipment alone is to be hired, particularly as part of a mix-and-match set with gear brought out from the UK, the production needs to be quite sure about compatibility of systems. Simple matters like finding out if the usual voltage is 110 volts or 240 volts or if the television standard is PAL, NTSC or one of the varieties of SECAM is vital as is making sure that appropriate film or tape stock is easily available. Everything will depend on the country concerned and the standards of work regarded as acceptable vary wildly. The only hope of estimating the skills of the foreign technicians or the reliability of the available equipment is to talk to a director who has previously worked in the countries concerned or to operate in conjunction with a local office of a British company.

In the event of contracting foreign technicians, the contract must be worked out in advance which is probably only practicable through a local broadcast company or a resident British office. Local freelance crews may have very fixed ideas about working hours and conditions. There may be charges for every kilometre travelled, every meal on location, and for local ideas of overtime.

Consumable items such as microphone batteries, videotape stock and simple things like adhesive tape and aerosols can be exorbitantly priced in many countries. It is worth taking a case of sundries of everything down to paper clips and ballpoint pens (useful as currency in some countries) despite excess baggage charges. The camera operator must decide about equipment hire. It might be quite acceptable in most circumstances to hire lights and electricians locally but probably not cameras.

The fixer

Finally, the most important additional member of the team, the local fixer.

In any unfamiliar country it will be essential to have a fixer who knows the television business and is fluent in both English and the local languages. Only a local resident will be able to explain how to navigate a production around the inevitable problems of obtaining permits, fees and contracts, police procedures, and the etiquette of dealing with contributors and officialdom. Fixers come in all shapes and conditions. Many cities in the USA and elsewhere have film commissions whose very function is to smooth the way for visiting crews. The main British broadcast companies have offices or representatives in the major European cities and will be able to suggest freelance fixers, though the best expedient of all will be to talk to a director who has worked in the country in question and can recommend someone by name.

In some authoritarian states you may have no choice about having a fixer as a condition of being allowed in and given accreditation may be to accept an appointed shadow. If the subject is non-controversial and the appointed fixer has some knowledge of the needs of television, this may be all to the good. If the topic is regarded as being in any way sensitive, however, the main function of your fixer is to be your minder with an eye to preventing you seeing what you came for or talking to whom you want. In this case the director is into a familiar cat-and-mouse game of using the fixers when appropriate and getting rid of them when not. Some authoritarian countries are usually in thrall to mind numbing procedures for permissions. For example to shoot a tourist infested mosque in Cairo will require television accreditation as well as written permits from three ministries for three separate set-ups: from the street (Police), exteriors (Antiquities) and interiors (Religious Affairs).

In most locations though it will be up to the production to find and contract their own fixer and unless a thoroughly reliable recommendation has been obtained in advance this will require a recce by the director or a researcher or production manager.

Whatever the cost of extra air fares an efficient recce and the discovery of the right fixer is an essential pre-condition to a successful shoot overseas.

A freelance fixer might be a journalist stringer, a trained production manager, the owner of a travel agency or even a taxi driver. Good fixers' names tend to be passed from production team to production team. If personal contacts do not suffice, a look at back copies of the television trade press such as *Broadcast*, the BBC house paper *Ariel*, and *Televisual* will have articles on productions in foreign parts and may even mention fixers by name. A telephone call to the appropriate production office should lead to helpful advice.

Warning
There are countries where it is normal for officials to supplement their salaries by exacting contributions from their victims. An oiled palm may be expected not only by traffic policemen and hotel receptionists but museum directors and the managers of airline offices. The methods used range in subtlety from robbery at gun point to the suggestion of cash contributions to a vaguely specified charity. The most usual symptom, often beginning at an airport ticket desk or immigration barrier, is the discovery of unexplained irregularities which will cause protracted delays or even detention of persons or equipment.

A stubborn display of apparent ignorance about what is going on will often wear down the hopeful extortioner. Otherwise how you deal with the situation will depend on the strength of moral principles, the urgency of the deadlines and the depth of your pocket.

Recceing abroad: a checklist

A recce is always desirable and usually essential. The BBC suggests 12 basic sets of information which their production managers should look for.

- Weather conditions at the proposed time of shooting.
- Local events and holidays which might affect the production.
- Suitable accommodation.
- Availability of transport.
- Situation for contracting performers (or contributors in factual programmes).

- Local banks (and currency exchange and money transfer problems).
- Shipping agents if needed.
- Local staff and union requirements.
- Official filming permits.
- Relations with the police.
- Restrictions on filming (censorship and security concerns in factual programmes).
- Bribery, corruption and the black economy.

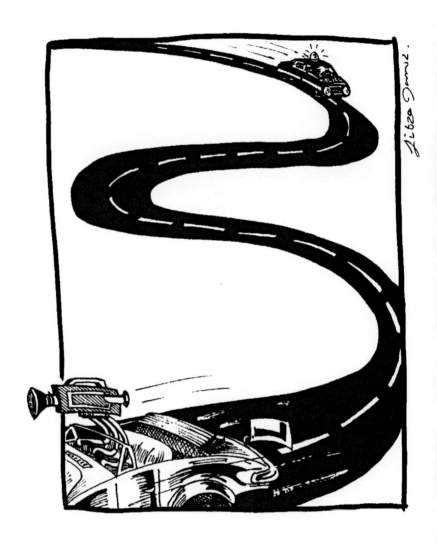

3
ROAD AND RAIL

On the road

Many of the most seductive shots which suggest themselves to a director on location will involve transport by land, sea and air. Television is, after all, about moving pictures. Unhappily some of the most tragic disasters in the history of film-making have resulted from the reckless use of moving vehicles and the hazards are sometimes not obvious. Police liaison has been mentioned above as always being desirable. With any shooting involving the public highway, it is essential. Road traffic regulations do not make any exceptions for television crews, but if the police and highway authorities are sensibly approached they may suspend the regulations briefly over certain stretches of highway for short periods.

In some locations such as central London, you will be restricted to times which will minimise potential disruption so expect to receive full cooperation, but only in the small hours of a Sunday morning.

The police will be keenly interested in anything which might disrupt the traffic flow but might volunteer officers to accompany the unit and help ensure that the difficulties and dangers are minimised.

No member of the unit is authorised to flag down or stop traffic. If this is apparently essential during takes, a police presence is vital. If the police cannot volunteer manpower, you may have to offer to pay a fee for an officer in the same way that football stadiums do.

The police may sometimes consider closing lanes or minor roads or temporarily diverting traffic for filming. It does no harm to ask.

Ambitious productions can try another approach in rural areas. The appropriate local highways authority might be asked to issue a 'Temporary Road Closure Order' but this would entail a notice period of at least six weeks.

There are often stretches of motorway or highway under repair or construction these days which are not open to traffic but which may be suitable for filming. On-site enquiries about permissions to use these can be made.

Driving on the public highway involves all the normal obligations of insurance, tax, driving licences and MOT tests. Drivers and passengers have to wear seat-belts even if this gives a rather comic edge to your robbery get-away sequence.

Many domestic car insurance policies specifically exclude cover for cars used for filming. Cover has to be arranged. Hire cars are a better option so long as the rental company is aware of what is envisaged and the models available are appropriate to the plot. Large production companies normally have specific insurance coverage. Corporate video producers may hope to ensure suitable cover through a sponsoring company's motor insurance policy.

As a simple safety precaution, all unit members should be issued with highly reflective waistcoats or protective clothing.

> **Hint**
> For dramatic reasons it may be necessary to use a false number plate. In factual programmes the true identity of a vehicle may have to be disguised.
>
> The use of false number plates on the public highway is illegal. The use of an invented number plate can give rise to terrible legal complications if an imaginatively chosen number happens to belong to a real vehicle and the depiction is in any way defamatory to the owner (see Chapter 14). Non-operative registration numbers can be obtained from:
>
> **The Driving and Vehicle Licensing Centre**
> Swansea SA99 1AB

Private roadways

Private roadways are often easy to locate. There are a large number of surfaced roads and tracks owned by the Forestry Commission and private landowners. Water companies own large stretches of countryside with private roadways. There are dozens of small airfields, many of Second World War vintage, which are rarely used and have miles of runway and perimeter track, now privately owned. Quarry companies own large areas which share with those run by the Army the advantage that nothing a television company can do is likely to cause any more damage. A private road is contractually the same as a private house. The production company still has to ascertain ownership, avoid trespass, probably offer a facility fee and indemnify the landlords against accidents or damage.

Although increasing areas of land once administered by public authorities are being privatised, location suggestions might begin with:

The Forestry Commission of Great Britain
231 Corstophine Road
Edinburgh EH12 7AT

The Countryside Commission
John Dower House
Crescent Place
Cheltenham
Gloucestershire GL50 3RA

Many private landowners are members of the following:

The Country Landowners Association
16 Belgrave Square
London SW1X 8PQ

The Woodland Trust
Autumn Park
Grantham
Lincolnshire NG31 6LL

Categories of vehicles

Vehicles may be used in several ways, and the differences may effect both fees and insurance.

As a dressing property

The vehicle is static and essentially part of the scenery, particularly common in period drama and documentary dramatisations. This frequently demands cars of a specific model and date. Suitable vehicles, properly insured, can be hired from commercial hire firms or specialist motor collections and museums, most of which are accustomed to working with advertising and television companies. Vintage vehicles will usually be delivered by trailer and will come with their own drivers and possibly with mechanics as well. If the vehicle is to be brought into a studio or other confined space, the petrol tank must be drained to contain less than a pint of fuel and all fire and safety precautions observed.

As an action property

The car is to be driven in shot. The question arises 'who is to do the driving?' Actors should be let loose on cars with the greatest of reluctance, even in the most carefully controlled location. Even a dramatic sequence of slamming the door on a stationary vehicle can result in awful damage. If the scene demands anything other than the simplest manoeuvres, a double or stunt driver should be considered. With veteran cars the driver may have to be the one supplied with the car. Several of the agencies which supply prop vehicles employ drivers who belong to Equity. This solves the problems of asking people to appear in costume or to take direction (see Extras pp. 71–73) but if the vehicle in question is a tracked vehicle or combine harvester, the available drivers may not have any experience of performing.

Location units often hire professional drivers and this might appear to offer a solution. Be aware though of Road Transport Regulations. Regardless of how busy they seem, the regulations for driving on public roads stipulate a minimum of 11 hours per day 'rest period' for each driver (reducible to nine hours for not more than three days in a week if compensated for during the following week). As the drivers will typically be the first to start and the last to finish, their duty periods tend to be long. Actual driving time is limited to nine, occasionally ten, hours per day. Driving off-road or on private premises does not count towards the legal driving hours but it does count as 'other work'. In other words using your contracted drivers as anything extra will involve extra fees. For reference contact:

 The Film Unit Drivers Guild
Guild House
51 North Road
London SW19 1AQ

As a camera platform

Big drama shoots or crews covering racing events will need to hire some of the vast range of specialist camera vehicles and camera mounts available.

The low-budget production will have to improvise. Some camera operators have their own adapted vehicles, or anyhow will not object to using their own transport for tracking shots through a roof opening or the open tailgate of an estate car or van. But agreement must be reached well in advance and sensible safety measures taken. The use of hand held shots taken from or inside a moving car is limited. The more elegant solution is to mount both prop car and camera on the bed of a low loader and to tow them. If car shots with a moving background of real traffic and an identifiable location are essential, a low loader is the one way that moving shots on the public highway can be achieved, always assuming that the problem cannot be resolved through video effects in post-production.

In recent years there have also been spectacular developments in miniature cameras to the extent that they can now be mounted on or in items as diverse as cricket stumps, drivers' helmets, birds in flight and parts of the human anatomy. These may be hired from the major equipment companies which will also stipulate whether specialist operators are required as well as make clear any insurance implications.

More traditional camera equipment may be used. There are a huge variety of specialist mounts for attaching cameras, and even camera operators, to the sides of motor vehicles, but not all mounts are adaptable to all camera bodies and a specialist rig may have to be constructed so decisions about driving shots ought to made in good time. Using camera mounts will involve hiring a grip to both install the rig safely and ensure its smooth operation. Trying to cut corners and operate with a lash-up is a recipe for disaster. An improperly set up camera mount can damage paint work or badly bend doors and side panels. An unsafe camera flying off a moving car will result in a hefty bill if not injury to those present. Cameramen will sometimes refuse to work with any mounting more sophisticated than a standard tripod without a grip. Paying for a grip can be money well spent as operations will be speeded up enormously.

A cheap and cheerful solution is a limpet mount which is no more than a large rubber sucker and plate for attaching a camera, usually to the top of a car bonnet facing the windscreen. The need for well-lashed safety lines is obvious. One limitation is the flimsy steel of many cars' construction which may result in the metal flexing up and down whilst the car is in motion. Removal of the sucker might also remove a ring of paint work from older cars.

Note for film buffs
Why is a grip called a grip?
Because in the early days of movies the director had a driver who also humped his bags (grips) around locations. When an extra pair of hands were needed to push a camera around the cameraman would 'send for the grip'. These days a good grip is a highly specialised technician.

On the railways

Britain has a great selection of railway societies, steam clubs, and several working steam museums, transport collections as well as sections of commercially run private railways and tramways.

Historic rolling stock is always in demand for period drama productions.

Documentary productions will best afford access to these historic lines if they keep their demands to times outside holiday periods and to when enthusiasts are planning a display or excursion. It costs time and money to get up steam on any old engine, whether a locomotive or a static pumping engine.

Private railways will usually be eager to help, out of enthusiasm, for hard cash, or a mixture of both. The same procedures should be followed as for any other location and the actual logistics worked out carefully with someone who can estimate how long various aspects will take and who is aware of any operational or safety problems.

The use of operational public transport raises different problems.

British Rail

At the moment of writing, British Rail is being privatised and dismembered into a number of operating companies, which will run the rolling stock and provide the services, and Railtrack, which will administer the railway itself. Where this will leave a producer or director in future is anyone's guess. Because of the privatisation upheaval productions are advised to begin all enquiries locally.

Currently the procedure is to contact the manager of the relevant station who will liaise with the local BR Public Affairs Office. If there are no objections to the filming, a standard application form will be sent requesting details of camera positions, lighting, parking and so on. British Transport Police will also be involved from this stage on to ensure that the very detailed railway by-laws involving public safety are observed. Some of the dramatic train shots you will have seen a dozen times before may these days be vetoed on safety grounds. Three or four weeks' minimum notice is advised, as is a detailed technical recce with a railway official.

In some circumstances the production company may be permitted to dress a station in period style and some of British Rail's own historic rolling stock may be hired. There are of course a number of small stations which are rarely used, not counting the many rural ones which are redundant or have been sold off to private owners. British Rail also owns some magnificent terminus buildings, vast areas of sidings and even abandoned workshop buildings in urban areas.

It is possible to obtain permission to film on trains. Remember that the very pliant laws of trespass do not apply to railways and railway property and attempts to shoot on either without a permit will lead not just to a request to leave but quite probably arrest and detention by the Transport Police. For production purposes a whole compartment or carriage can be reserved, exceptionally even an entire train.

> **Hint**
> More than one director has worked out his or her train shots in detail but forgotten the details of how to get the performers or crew back.
>
> Return trains or waiting road transport need to be confirmed. The performer who is seen bidding a tearful farewell on a departing train will not be impressed if instead of stopping at the next station, the particular service is non-stop to Glasgow or there is no return service for three hours.

London Underground

London Underground is the most difficult of all rail services to use for filming.

Any attempt to shoot without permission, even on a forecourt or station entrance, will lead to a speedy expulsion by the management and probable Transport Police intervention.

Station managers are not authorised to grant permissions.

London Underground has a film facilities administrator who is the first point of contact for obtaining permission. He or she will then clear everything with the relevant line managers. The safety implications of shooting on a crowded metropolitan station or in a busy carriage are obvious and permission may only be granted during certain hours, on certain sections of track, or after the last service at night.

London Underground operates this office on a commercial basis so there may be detailed enquiries about technical resources, script or storyboard, and numbers involved. A facility fee will be calculated on the basis of this information. Enquiries should be made to:

London Underground Limited
55 Broadway
London SW1H 0BD

The Glasgow Underground

Glasgow Underground has been far more welcoming to television companies than London Underground and has the advantage of compactness of scale in both the railway and the bureaucracy, though of course like all metro systems it is immediately identifiable to observant viewers.

The main proviso is that all productions must first complete a detailed indemnity form against all injury or damage to property arising out of the filming and a commitment to observe all safety precautions and instructions from railway staff. Detailed proposals should be addressed to:

The Press Office
The Strathclyde Passenger Transport Executive
12 West George St.
Glasgow G2 1HN

The Tyne and Wear Metro and the Merseyrail Underground

The Newcastle area Metro has become used to television crews and operates in a similar manner to the Glasgow Underground.

Crews may expect to be accompanied at all times whilst on Metro property and to be strictly supervised. Unlike British Rail and London Underground, however, these smaller transit systems do not own much of the land immediately adjacent to the lines and so shooting close to the metro needs alternative permissions but has less stringent requirements for safety supervision.

There is a similar Metro system covering the Liverpool area. Permission to film on either of these two systems should be applied for from:

Tyne and Wear Passenger Transport Executive
Metro Offices
South Gosforth Industrial Estate
Newcastle upon Tyne NE3 1XW

Merseyrail Electrics
Rail House
Lord Nelson Street
Liverpool L1 1JF

4

MESSING ABOUT IN BOATS

The thought of filming on or about the sea can be wonderfully seductive.

It is not within the scope of this book to go into the artistic and technical perils of working on water but suffice it to say that often the most hard won and ravishing 'sails in the sunset' shots finish up on the cutting room floor. A thousand corporate videos are witness to the fact that something as exciting to the participants as power-boat racing or water-skiing becomes a repetitious bore on the small screen and are not improved by adding a pounding percussive music track.

It is also too easy to over-estimate the amount of footage and the number of shots which can be achieved in a day. On water everything takes twice as long as on land. Working with boats is very different from working with road vehicles. If the production team has nobody with direct experience of working on water then it will be essential to admit ignorance and plan the shoot with someone who knows what they are talking about. A recce is essential.

Before you start consider carefully the points in the following checklist:

- Get a book of local tide tables and make sure that the recce takes account both of whether the tide will be high or low and whether it will be ebbing or flowing at the proposed times of shooting. If shooting is to take place on more than one day take account of how the state of the tide changes daily. Particularly if you are working in estuaries, you must know the difference between spring and neap tides as a recce at the time of high water spring tide will give a very different impression to high water neaps a fortnight later. Those who think that spring tides refers to the season of the year and not the phase of the moon should definitely not plan a maritime production without a minder.
- Check the probable weather and visibility conditions. On some coasts morning sea mists are quite predictable and will prevent early shooting. Mist can also be affected by tides. As a result,

long shots may have to be scheduled for late in the day. Weather conditions will have to be regularly monitored from the day before the intended shoot and throughout the filming period. A problem is that coastal waters often have weather patterns all of their own. It may pour with rain on shore and be brilliant sunshine a mile out at sea, or vice versa. The 24-hour Meteorological Office forecasts will give approximate conditions for land. The shipping forecast broadcast by the BBC is particularly useful.

- Work from a large-scale Ordnance Survey map and, if putting to sea, an Admiralty chart. With these two maps it should be possible to get a good idea of likely camera positions as well as the logistical problems of getting from A to B both on shore and on the water. A surprising number of ferries marked on maps have either ceased business or work only in the summer.

- Decide how many boats will be needed. For most maritime sequences two vessels will be needed; one to film and one to be filmed from. To get a useful range of shots this means two cameras, one on each boat. But in addition it may be necessary to have a third boat to act as a safety tender or to ferry crews and equipment from set-up to set-up or from boat to boat.

- Check the hours of sunrise and sunset and particularly the changing position of the sun during the day as this will define which shots will be possible between which hours. Last minute manoeuvring to get the camera on the sunlit side of another boat or get rid of an obtrusive background takes time and can play havoc with continuity, particularly where boats under sail are involved.

- Plan for mechanical problems either of the camera equipment or of the boats involved. Outboard motors are notoriously misanthropic. Salt spray and electronic equipment do not go together and protective covers are essential. Filming on the water does not allow the option of popping back to get a couple of microphone batteries or a spare cable.

- Work out the communications problems. You must not clutter up the ship-to-shore airwaves with your chatter so walkie-talkies of an approved frequency are essential.

- Find out if any of the team are not good sailors. Cameramen, even if they are keen yachtsmen, can become very sick if asked to look at a viewfinder for a long period whilst at sea.

Wherever possible the director should have Plan B at the ready if Plan A falls apart for reasons of sea conditions. On the appointed day it may be impossible to set out at all, or changing weather may make it necessary to break and run for harbour. It is unwise to argue with your skipper over these decisions.

Boat hire

Hiring craft takes one of three forms.

- The production hires the craft to be sailed by members of the team.
- The craft is chartered for the production complete with skipper and crew.
- The craft is contracted to appear in the production but without camera or performers on board.

A boat chartered without skipper becomes a 'property' of the production. It is therefore the responsibility of the production team to return the craft in an undamaged state and to agree hire and fuel charges. Third-party insurance for boats regularly put out to hire may not be valid for filming purposes and it is the responsibility of the producer to verify this.

Unless the subject matter demands it, it is usually not worthwhile trying to save money by self-crewing a craft and filming. Shooting from boats is likely to involve more complex manoeuvres than those normally encountered by a weekend sailor. Even the seemingly most straightforward shots can raise problems, particularly if the production unit members are not thoroughly familiar with the operation of the vessel and the navigational rules. Hiring a canal narrow boat for a day on five feet of water sounds foolproof but a shooting day is no time to start learning how to operate bridges or use a lock windlass.

Chartering a vessel with a skipper and crew means that the production team travel as passengers in the eyes of the law. In production terms the boat is a location facility and should be regarded in the same way as hired premises on land. In these circumstances check the following:

- Is the vessel licensed to carry the intended number of passengers?
- If the owner of the craft fully insured against damage to the hull, machinery and equipment and if not, does he or she agree to operate entirely at his own risk?
- Is there any third-party liability which extends to yourselves as passengers?

Many ports and harbours have their own boatmen's association which is fully licensed for most eventualities and are fully up on safety and insurance matters. In fact, in some well-used marine locations, television productions are faced by a well-inflated set of charges fixed by the cartel. In other locations, such as the tidal reaches of the Thames at London, you may only shoot from vessels chartered from licensed watermen.

Trouble is only likely to arise when a production either charters or accepts the offer of privately owned craft without checking the implications if things go wrong, or when for documentary purposes it is necessary to operate with commercial craft other than those licensed for passengers, for example inshore fishing boats.

Hiring a craft and crew to perform as part of the action involves paying an appearance fee. The owner must agree that he or she accepts full liability for both vessel and crew. It is still essential though to go through what is required in as much detail as possible, even to the extent of agreeing a story board in advance. The skipper may have as vague an idea about the demands of filming as the director has about the problems of navigation.

The skipper will rely upon his or her own judgement about the reasonableness of requests. But if the director demands unsafe or unwise manoeuvres, the skipper complies, and an accident then ensues, both the skipper and the director are liable to criminal prosecution.

Safety afloat

Passenger-carrying charter vessels should automatically carry the regulation complement of life jackets, life rafts and fire safety equipment. Not all craft though may be fully equipped to meet the demands of filming nor may skippers anticipate the sort of atypical demands a director or camera operator might make, so a safety audit is important before the shoot takes place.

Safety audit

- Does every single member of the unit have a life jacket and know how to use it? This is as important for inland waters as the high seas.
- Do performers, camera operators or equipment need additional safety lines to achieve the shots required?
- Are there any non-swimmers in the unit or performers in costumes which might encumber them in the water? If either case applies, special precautions must be taken.
- Does the shoot justify having a diver dressed and ready to go in at all times and is there a member of the unit with a

knowledge of lifesaving and resuscitation?
- Are there adequate fire extinguishers aboard, particularly if any special effects are being considered?
- If shooting from shore, quay side or canal bank, are there life buoys and lines within easy access?
- Before setting out, which authorities should be notified of your plans? These may involve harbourmasters, HM Coastguard or the Customs and Excise if you are leaving territorial waters.

Health warning
Many inland waterways and harbours are heavily polluted. A particular concern of late has been Weils disease in canals with large rat populations. If there is the likelihood of a soaking, or the immersion of any of the crew or performers, it is as well to inquire about any health risk with the National Rivers Authority. In some circumstances a laboratory analysis of the water may be asked for and medical advice counselled.

Coastal waters

The British coast is comprehensively covered by emergency services which coordinate to provide the SAR (search and rescue) services through HM Coastguard, the Royal Navy, the Royal Air Force and the Royal National Lifeboat Institution. Each of these may be important to productions even if things do not go wrong. Naval or coastal Air Force bases may be able to advise on local weather prospects.

The RNLI is always eager to assist film makers to portray its work since the lifeboats are staffed by volunteers and is financed by public subscriptions. Lifeboats will not offer their services as camera platforms or safety boats. They will expect the production to be fully indemnified and will expect it to meet any incidental costs of the shoot. It is expected that the unit will make a generous contribution to the funds of the lifeboat. Apart from this, the bo'sun of the nearest lifeboat may be one of the best sources of information about local maritime problems during a recce.

HM Coastguard coordinates the other services through six regional centres. Some of these centres have specialist responsibilities for liaison with off-shore oil installations, operating cross-channel navigation information services or handling worldwide satellite communications.

A further service is represented by the General Lighthouse

Authorities which comprises Trinity House (responsible for lighthouses and navigation marks in English and Welsh waters), the Northern Lighthouse Board (for Scottish waters) and the Commissioners of Irish Lights (which covers both Northern Ireland and the Irish Republic).

Unfortunately for film makers most of the old lighthouses and island lights are today remote controlled installations without keepers, but where local staff remain, they can be an invaluable source of information. Permission to shoot on lighthouses is possible although access is often a problem. Detailed information may be obtained from:

The Department of Transport (Coastguards)
2 Marsham Street
London SW1P 3EB

Royal National Lifeboat Institute
West Quay Road
Poole
Dorset BH15 1HZ

The Northern Lighthouse Board
84 George Street
Edinburgh EH2 3DA

The Commissioners of Irish Lights
16 Lower Pembroke Street
Dublin 2
Republic of Ireland

Trinity House Lighthouse Service
Trinity House
Tower Hill
London EC3N 4DH

Most small harbours employ a resident harbourmaster paid by the local government authority, and private marinas have their own administration. Each may be expected to levy berthing charges and in the case of most harbours a charge for each time a craft enters or leaves harbour waters. Larger harbours are run by statutory port authorities.

Ports are busy commercial enterprises and permission to shoot on shore or sea within their jurisdiction must be obtained in advance. Most are members of one of two associations which should be approached in the first instance:

Associated British Ports
150 Holborn
London EC1N 2LR

The British Ports Association
Africa House
64–78 Kingsway
Holborn
London WC2B 6AH

Inland waters

Most navigable inland waterways come under the authority of:

British Waterways
Willow Grange
Church Road
Watford WD1 3QA

There is no general right of access or navigation for inland waters in England and Wales although different rules prevail in Scotland and Ireland. The overall regulatory body for English rivers, lakes and reservoirs is:

The National Rivers Authority
Eastbury House
30̇034 Albert Embankment
London SE1 7TL

and for Scotland:

The Scottish River Purification Boards Association
1 South Street
Perth PH2 8NJ

Warning
Whilst filming at sea do NOT:

- simulate any kind of incident without full prior consultation with all the harbour and emergency services;
- fire off distress rockets or ignite flares;
- hoist incorrect flags or give misleading signals;
- use smoke or flame effects at sea;
- ignore navigation marks;
- enact drowning, capsizing or cliff accidents where members of the public may be deceived.

Tomfoolery leading to the needless launch or a lifeboat or helicopter will not be appreciated by the rescue services.

5
UP AND AWAY

Aerial shots have the same sort of appeal as sailing sequences for many directors. There is no doubt that shots from an aircraft can enormously enhance a programme. But the failure to plan any aerial sequence properly, or a lack of awareness of the limitations of a particular aircraft can result in a lot of disappointment, and a great deal of expense. It ought also to be patently obvious that flying can also be a very hazardous activity.

The three likeliest ways by which a production is going to get airborne is by:

- using aeroplanes or helicopters belonging to the armed forces or other organisation such as the police or an oil company;
- by hiring the services of a company specialising in aerial photography;
- by making *ad hoc* arrangements with individual pilots or flying companies.

Helicopters are usually the best choice of aircraft, but they do not come cheap. Approximate costs quoted by the British Film Commission in 1995 were:

Single engine helicopters	£400–500 per flying hour
Twin engine helicopters	£700–900 per flying hour
Very large helicopters	£1500–3500 per flying hour

You only pay for the time when the engine is running, though there is usually a minimum fee of a few hours. This will include getting the helicopter to and from location and any time spent returning to an airfield for re-fuelling. Filming dates and times may have to be organised around the availability of a helicopter already working in a particular area. It is often suggested that in addition to the pilot, the production hires a flight mechanic. The mechanic will be responsible for any modifications to the aircraft such as removing doors or windows or moving seating, and for setting up camera mounts and safety lines.

In the case of craft not specifically adapted for aerial photography the camera operator may have to film through an open door, suitably attached to a safety harness.

Specialist firms will supply camera mounts and these range from basic rubber vibration mounts through fixed or tilting belly mounts or nose mounts, through to balance mounts of various sophistication. There are computer-operated gyro-stabilised camera spheres, which require specialist operators. As with most things you get what you pay for but the top end of the market is likely to be within the reach of only the most extravagant television drama, feature films or more commonly, cinema and television commercials.

A recent innovation is the midget-sized remote-controlled hovercam, which can carry up to a 35 mm Arri film camera. A five-foot long hovering camera mount is uniquely attractive, but it has its limitations, particularly where safety is involved. Bad weather will ground it, and to insure against this possibility is advisable but expensive. Fees range from £2000 to £4000 per day.

Fixed-wing planes are subject to a far greater variability in costs, depending on the kind of aeroplane concerned and how the craft is chartered. The minimum rate is likely to be the hourly rate for flying lessons at the airfield concerned. Few light aircraft can accommodate more than a couple of passengers and often there is room for only one, plus the camera equipment. It should be realised that, due to the nature of flying, the camera operator has very little choice about getting shots once airborne. In effect the pilot is the cameraman and director combined and unless the very sophisticated mounts are hired, all the camera operator can achieve will be to hold a static wide angle shot from a fixed position whilst the pilot positions the craft for the optimum height and angle. The geometry of many small aircraft is such that it is often impossible to film without parts of the wing or undercarriage appearing in shot, even if a side door is removed. Shooting inside a crowded cockpit from behind a pilot is terribly restricted and such shots are often best mocked up on the ground and inter-cut with the flying sequences.

The director must prepare a list of shots, preferably with the help of a storyboard, in consultation with the pilot. A dummy run before shooting will be money well spent. As with any kind of action filming, the director has to be clear about crossing the line of action and determine whether the action is to be left to right or right to left across the screen. The position of the sun must be noted. A low sun into the lens is to be avoided but summer landscapes often show their features to best advantage early or late in the day when the shadows pick out the relief. The angle of the sun may also determine whether aircraft shadow over the ground can be avoided.

Light aircraft must be balanced so the deployment of the film crew and equipment has to be set. Once airborne it is no time to start shifting seats or positions. Communication in the cockpit is probably best achieved by a pre-arranged set of hand signals, there is no scope for discussions about shot sizes in the air.

All equipment such as spare magazines, batteries or tape cassettes must be readily to hand but also well secured. A loose piece of equipment could jam one of the aircraft controls.

Last-minute improvisation will quite rightly result in the pilot refusing to perform the manoeuvres requested.

The regulatory body for all civil flying activity is the Civil Aviation Authority (CAA). The CAA is responsible for clearing the use of aircraft and airspace for filming. The permutations of filming requirements, aircraft type and air traffic considerations are so varied that specific clearances or exemptions may be obligatory for any shoot. It should be noted that whilst shooting, aircraft may not fly closer than:

- 500 feet to people, vehicles or buildings;
- 1500 feet over built up areas;
- 3000 feet over crowds;
- 750 feet over Greater London except directly over the Thames;
- 1500 feet within one kilometre of any royal palace (see pp. 7–8).

Helicopters with doors off may not fly faster than 70 mph.

With permitted low-level or stunt flying no ground personnel should be within 500 feet of the craft or its projected flight path. Flying over built-up areas may necessitate a twin engine aeroplane. It should be remembered that airspace around both civil and military airports is tightly restricted.

The CAA has formulated a comprehensive list of regulations concerning safety in the air in collaboration with the Television Safety Services of the BBC. These cover both helicopters and fixed wing aircraft as well as the use of microlights, gliders, balloons, airships, power chutes, hang gliders, parachutes and model helicopters and aircraft.

CAA regulations may vary in each case depending on both the nature of the shooting and the chosen locality. It is strongly recommended that before any camera or performer is sent aloft all the details are checked for clearance with one of the following:

The Civil Aviation Authority
Safety Regulation Group
Aviation House
South Area Gatwick Airport
Gatwick, West Sussex RH6 0YR

The Civil Aviation Authority (Scotland)
Aviation House
31 Pinkhill
Edinburgh EH12 7BD

The CAA will also advise on the use of foreign registered aircraft and the regulatory bodies for aerial filming overseas.

It is the responsibility of the television production company as well as of the aircraft operator to ensure that CAA clearances have been granted. There are basic considerations which must be taken into account if a production is stay within the law, or indeed stay in one piece.

Pilots

There are three categories of licence for aircraft pilots:

- Private Pilot's Licence (PPL);
- Commercial Pilot's Licence (CPL);
- Airline Transport Pilot's Licence (ATPL).

Only the last two categories may fly for commercial reward. Carrying a camera crew counts as public transport and so such flights must also be covered by an Air Operator's Certificate. An exception is if the camera is on a fixed mount and no passengers are carried in which case no Air Operator's Certificate is needed but the pilot must still hold a commercial licence.

The holder of a PPL may not fly for 'valuable consideration' although in return for an agreement over sharing fuel costs he or she might be asked to perform routine take-off, flying or landing routines for the camera.

The likelihood is that the flyer will be a member of a flying club, and it is likely that the first recourse for hiring a fixed-wing light aircraft will be a club whose instructors will hold commercial licences and whose insurance ought to cover filming requirements. In either case the production should make a few frank enquiries about the expertise as well as likely temperament of a pilot. Flyers tend to be scathing about the capacities of others and the old chestnut to keep in mind is 'There are old flyers, and there are bold flyers, but there are no old bold flyers.'

Insurance tip
It may be possible to enrol the camera crew as temporary members of a flying club to take advantage of their insurance schemes.

Aircraft

Aircraft themselves fall into four categories of air worthiness:

- Public transport: licensed to carry passengers.

- Aerial work (e.g. crop spraying): passengers may not be carried.
- Private use: no paying passengers or commercial work permitted.
- Special category/permit to fly: generally non-standard or vintage aircraft which require a special CAA dispensation to fly.

Any CAA dispensation should be obtained in writing and distributed both to all production and technical staff concerned and the insurers of the aircraft pilot and the production itself. All production staff have to be clear that they accept the risks involved in flying.

Equipment

Any radio equipment taken into an aircraft must be CAA approved which means that the frequencies must be cleared for airborne use. A small number of suitable frequencies have been allocated for the use of the BBC and ITV companies. Any technical equipment using radio frequencies should be given a ground check to make sure that there is no interference with the aircraft's control systems.

In the air

It is the responsibility of the pilot in every category of aircraft to make sure that all passengers are aware of the safety drill relevant to the make of plane, and the operation of safety equipment and harnesses. Over water it may be obligatory to wear life jackets at all times.

When air-to-air shots are required both pilots should be checked for experience of formation flying. It is essential that the aeroplane carrying the camera should keep to an agreed course and speed and that any manoeuvering should be done by the planes being filmed. The plane being filmed should never under fly the camera plane. Apart from making it impossible to get a shot, it is extremely dangerous.

On the ground

Even small airfields are a complex of various commercial enterprises. An airfield or airport management might grant permission to film and arrange the necessary liaison with air traffic control and local security. You may still have to negotiate separately for access and availability with the various flying schools, maintenance workshops, charter firms, shipping agents and so on.

Aeroplanes can be more dangerous on the ground than in the air. The following points should be made clear to all members of the production team:

- The pilot of a taxiing plane cannot see the ground immediately in front of the plane, or hear anything except through the earphones.
- There may be safety or security reasons for restricting or prohibiting filming from perimeter roads, runways or turning areas.
- Working near jet engines may require ear defenders.
- Nobody should approach the propeller of a still warm engine. A mere nudge could start it up.
- Television people should stick to their jobs and not try to give a help in man-handling aircraft on the ground. It is easy to do damage to a fuselage as well as ones self.

Helicopters can have special perils.

- Helicopters generate 'rotor wash', which blasts up grit and any light debris. On take off or landing the down draft can be very powerful. Equipment may have to be protected and personnel issued with eye protection.
- The blades of a helicopter are obviously hazardous, particularly the tail rotor, which can easily not be noticed until too late.
- Helicopters must never be approached from a downhill slope or departed from on an uphill one and an approach should always be made in the line of sight of the pilot.

The following points apply equally well to aeroplanes and helicopters:

- When filming through an open door both the camera operator and the equipment should be safely attached by safety lines and harnessed. Flying suits and life jackets should be worn by everyone.
- Matches and cigarette lighters should not be found anywhere near aviation fuel.

Insurance

Both personnel and equipment must be properly insured. If technical equipment is on hire the rental firm may classify aerial photography as an unacceptably hazardous activity and insist on special cover. This applies especially to work with helicopters. Normal life and accident insurance policies specifically exclude cover for aerial filming or travel by helicopter so everyone concerned needs to check. All aircraft are legally required to carry third-party insurance and it may be possible to get the production company additionally insured under this policy. The safest thing to do is to get the production unit's insurance company agreement in writing to the details of the projected flights. Any oversight or bending of CAA regulations can give the insurers the right to designate a flight illegal and therefore to declare the policy null and void. The BBC advises producers to confirm the insurance of any aircraft and expects a third-party indemnity of at least £5 million.

6

THE ARTISTES

Apart from some special styles of documentary, almost every production will need the services of actors or presenters. Even natural history films need someone to read commentary. Casting and working with performers can lead the unwary producer into a number of pitfalls.

Featured artists

Professional British actors and actresses will normally belong to British Actors' Equity and agreement between Equity and broadcast television companies ensure that the performers employed have Equity membership and are paid at least the negotiated minimum rates. There are other categories of performer such as variety artists, dancers or circus entertainers who may or may not be Equity members. Following recent changes in trades union law, Equity no longer operates a closed shop for performers but normally Equity members will choose not to work alongside non-members. Whether your ambitions are Shakespearean or lean more towards jugglers or strippers, it is wise to confirm union conditions at an early stage. Certainly it is very unwise to propose mixing professional and amateur performers. If non-Equity performers have to be employed, for example as walk-ons or crowd artists (see pp. 71–73), they have to paid at the approved rates.

The bible of all casting directors is *Spotlight*, the directory of actors and actresses. *Spotlight* editions are revised annually and run to 11 mighty tomes with four for actors, four for actresses and extra volumes for children, new actors and actresses, and one specifically for television presenters. Each entry carries full details of the performer's experience, size and special aptitudes and in most cases a recent photograph. *Spotlight* is not for general sale though there is not a production company or actors agency which is not a subscriber. It is, however, available as a reference work in many libraries. Not all entries are from Equity members, for example presenters may have affiliation to the National Union of Journalists, or BECTU or no affiliation at all. Performers must pay a fee for their entry to be published but *Spotlight* is not a vanity press and will refuse entries from those involved only in amateur dramatics or who are not considered to be serious applicants.

Most performers have theatrical agents who are listed under each entry. The actors who do not may be contacted c/o *Spotlight* which will forward mail. Approaches ought to be made through the agent, but a personal approach can be worthwhile, particularly if the production in running on a shoestring budget or the director is set on one particular performer. One of the jobs of the agent is to jack up fees and maintain the market value of those on the books. On the other hand few actors or actresses can rely upon a steady supply of contracts and may take the attitude that it is better to take a poorly paid assignment than not to work at all. An interesting sounding role from a promising new director can look like an investment in the future even to a well-established 'name'.

Trying to be too clever by half and by-passing the agent can, however, get you into trouble. An informal approach still has contractual implications if it goes beyond a cautious availability check. If the approach takes the lines of 'Sir Ralph, would you be free to play King Lear between the twelfth and fifteenth?' and the good knight says yes you have made a verbal contract. If you then change your mind and employ Sir John instead you will be liable to pay a cancellation fee. As Sam Goldwyn said: 'A verbal statement ain't worth the paper it's written on', but a lot of trouble can be avoided by a properly written confirmation of an offer of work followed by a negotiated contract. This applies even if the contract is for no more than a one-off payment for a voice on an in-house corporate video.

A word of advice

Pleading poverty will not always get the desired response, particularly from actors and presenters in the public eye and ear. Performers who will give their services for a pittance to a worthwhile stage production may greatly bump up their fees for appearing in facile commercials or corporate productions.

Many television presenters can more than double their salaries by such work.

The reason is that many corporate clients seem to think that the appearance of a broadcast television personality gives professional credibility to their videos, and advertising agencies seek out the voices of performers currently appearing in popular programmes as implicit endorsement for their products.

It will pay to shop around through the pages of *Spotlight*. Public celebrity is a transient thing and the pages are full of first-rate performers who will be available for a reasonable reward.

Productions for broadcast naturally involve detailed provisos about repeat fees and secondary exploitation or through cable, satellite or videogram. Independent producers should seek advice from either of their professional associations, PACT for broadcasters, and IVCA for corporate and closed circuit productions, both of which have model contracts available.

There is nowhere in the world with such an abundance of excellent trained actors and actresses than the British Isles which, unfortunately for them, makes it very much of a buyers' market for producers.

Walk-ons, crowd artistes, supporting artists, stand-ins and doubles

There is a rigid line drawn between 'featured artists' and the various categories of walk-ons and extras. The matter is complicated superficially by the fact there are two bodies which negotiate employment for extras, Equity and the Film Artistes Association (FAA), and slightly different terminology and definitions are used in each case.

The Film Artistes Association has its roots in the feature film industry and is basically metropolitan. It represents extras used at any of the London-area film studios and has terms negotiated with PACT for all television productions made within 40 miles of Charing Cross.

Equity is the representative for extras nationwide and has negotiated conditions of work and pay for the BBC and most other broadcast companies as well as productions by PACT independents outside London.

Both organisations press for every kind of production to use its best endeavours to employ only union members whilst recognising that there are various circumstances when non-professional extras may have to be employed. As with featured actors and actresses, friction is only likely to arise where a production tries to mix professional performers with amateurs or unpaid members of the public to save money.

The representative bodies are:

 **British Actors Equity**
42 Cranbourne Street
London WC2H 7AP

Film Artistes Association
61 Marloes Road
London W8 6LF

The PACT/Equity definitions are:

- A *walk-on artist* appears either reacting to a featured actor or actress or in close-up impersonating an identifiable individual

or speaking a few unimportant words where the precise words do not have an effect on the script or the outcome of the story.
- A *background artist* appears in vision but is not required to give individual characterisation or speak any dialogue except crowd noises. The BBC term is *supporting artist* and the FAA's *crowd artiste*.

In a nutshell, the main difference is partly a slight difference in the initial daily rate, but mainly that walk-ons usually qualify for repeat payments and background artists do not. However, neither should be directed to deliver scripted dialogue or play a significant dramatic role, e.g. it is fine for a walk-on, dressed as a waiter or waitress, to deliver a menu, even to utter a few improvised words, but not for him or her to spill the wine on cue or make some scripted joke about the chef. If this situation is likely to arise the production is advised to hire an Equity-recognised actor. The minimum fees are not much greater and the director and writer will have complete flexibility during the shoot. You are not advised to ask an actor or actress to perform under the condition of an extra.

There are additional categories defined by the FAA:

- A *stand-in* is an artiste required to impersonate a featured actor or actress during plotting or rehearsals.
- A *double* is an artiste qualified to stand in during scenes, shots or set-ups where physical resemblance is not a requirement.
- A *lookalike double* is a stand-in who appears in shots in which a physical resemblance is important. There are also stunt doubles (see pp. 87–89).

In the main centres of population, extras of all categories are normally recruited through theatrical agents although in some locations advertising in *The Stage* or even local papers may be the best method. Some rural areas are more popular than others with productions simply because of a ready availability of Equity members in the locality, and transport or hotel costs can be minimised.

Extras are entitled to extra payments for either working under arduous conditions or for using special skills. Driving a vehicle or sitting on a horse classes as a special skill as does swimming or ballroom dancing and singing 'God Save The Queen' in unison. If the intention is to recreate the Battle of Mons at night and in real mud, extra payments for night shooting and demanding work will apply. Appearing topless (women) or nude (men) or simulating sexual intercourse (both) qualifies as a special skill or demanding work and special payments apply.

It is very important that extras and their agents are clearly briefed about what will be needed of them from the outset. Extras may be required to appear in their own suitable modern clothing but any subsequent cleaning will be at the cost of the production. Some walk-ons have their own private wardrobe, for example dinner jackets, ball gowns or military uniforms, and will wear these for a small additional fee which will be far cheaper than paying to hire and fit costumes.

Haircuts can be a bone of contention as performers may be asked to be shorn so as not to appear totally anachronistic in a period drama or ridiculously irrelevant to a social situation. Anything more than a mere trim might be counted as 'extreme for the fashions of the day' and unless the extra concerned has been contracted with a haircut clause, he or she is quite in order to refuse to comply and still expect to be paid.

Once contracted all categories must be paid in full whether or not on the day they are actually used in shot.

Using non-professionals

The employment of amateur performers or members of the public in dramatic situations has always been a grey area and there have been some spectacular disputes in the past. It has come to be accepted that there are circumstances where using non-professionals is unavoidable but the best advice is that a production should always endeavour only to employ them in circumstances where no extras are readily available or where the special skills demanded are uncommon. For example in fox hunting scenes it is accepted that a real hunt might be contracted rather that a collection of horse riding extras. There are a number of historic battle societies who not only have their own authentic costumes but can perform historically accurate drills and manoeuvres. These groups are accustomed to requests from all types of film, television and advertising companies and will have established fees and conditions.

In realistic modern drama or drama documentary it may be necessary to infiltrate professional extras amongst the actual public, for example in a football crowd or the audience at a political meeting. In such cases the director has to be very careful not to start giving specific direction to members of the public in the same manner as to the professional cast.

7

WORKING WITH CHILDREN

It is traditional theatrical advice never to work with children or animals. In view of the complications involved in employing juveniles any television director will agree that the advice still holds true. Anyone under school-leaving age, currently 16, counts as a child and also there are restrictions on the employment of 16 to 18 year olds who are in full-time education or asked to work abroad.

The legal framework is laid down by the Children's Performance Regulations 1968. A production employing children must establish:

- the number of days a child may perform in a year;
- the number of days a child may work in a week;
- the hours in a day a child may work;
- obligatory meal breaks and rest periods;
- arrangements for educational tuition over the working period;
- requirements for medical examination and supervision;
- the provision of suitable working and recreational conditions on location;
- the provision of chaperones or other supervision.

Foremost though is the problem of obtaining licences.

Any child being employed as a performer must be licensed by the local education authority for the district where the child lives. If the production is taking place elsewhere, the licence details will be forwarded to the relevant inspectors. The only exceptions to personal licensing are children from approved stage schools who are allowed to act for four days in any six months without an individual licence. Individual children are found in the children's edition of *Spotlight*. Other children may be allowed to appear as supporting artists for up to four odd days on designated school holidays only and subject to proper supervision, usually a parent or guardian if no matron or chaperone is present. Some professional extras are used to bringing their own children on appropriate assignments.

Licences must be applied for a minimum of 21 days, and ideally six weeks before the commencement of work. An application must have the approval of the legal parents or guardian and, where appropriate, the head teacher of the child's school. Applications must be accompanied by two passport-sized photographs and a copy of the child's birth certificate. The licence is then dependent on meeting the legal requirements and the maintenance of meticulously detailed records for the whole period of employment.

To guard against the exploitation of minors, the local education authority may also want to know about the fees agreed, who they are to be paid to and how they are going to be used. Under-16 year olds are not covered by Equity agreements.

Locations employing children are frequently visited by inspectors and any production ignoring or neglecting Home Office regulations is automatically liable to the cancellation of licences and criminal prosecution.

The permitted hours of work is complicated by compulsory earliest and latest start times. The Producers' Industrial Relations Service publishes the résumé documented in Table 7.1.

Table 7.1 Permitted daily hours of work, start times, educational provision and rest periods for minors

Age	Under five	Five to thirteen	Thirteen or over
Start times	09.30–16.30	09.00–16.30 (under ten) 09.00–17.00 (over ten)	09.00–19.00
Maximum hours allowed for rehearsal/ performance	5	7+	8
Maximum continuous hours allowed for rehearsal/ performance	+	+	1
Maximum total hours	2	3	3+
Minimum hours education provision (school days)	Nil	3	3
Rest and meal breaks	All times not working	A one-hour and a 15-minute break (in 3+ hours)	A one-hour and a 15-minute break (in 4 hours) or two one-hour and a15-minute break (in 8 hours)

Licences are not granted to any minor over 13 who has taken part in 80 days or more of performance in the previous 12 months, or to anyone under 13 with 40 days performance in the previous 12 months, not counting rehearsal days.

Applicants for a licence, who may be parents or theatrical agency as well as specific productions, may apply for a six-month 'open licence' which will allow television performance to a total of a specified number of days during the period, conditional of course on all the other conditions of licensing being observed. No children may work for more than five days in any seven including rehearsals.

Children on set or location must be supervised by a chaperone or matron who also must be licensed by the education authority and the number of children in the care of a single matron must not exceed 12. It is the licensed matron who is usually responsible for keeping the necessary daily records and ensuring the welfare of her charges both at work and travelling to and from home. Individual children may be accompanied by a parent or guardian and up to three children may be supervised by a privately engaged teacher in place of a matron. But is not permitted to foist several different children on the mother of one of them, or to ask adult members of the team to bring their kids along to a shoot whilst they are working, or to leave infants in the care of a kind wardrobe assistant between takes. These people do not count as proper chaperones.

To meet educational stipulations during school term times, a proper tutor may be needed in addition to a chaperone. All this raises accommodation problems. Suitable accommodation for recreation, refreshments and study have to be provided. This is self-preservation as well as regulation – a fractious five year old is no less a menace on set than a couple of bored teenage walk-ons.

If there is anything out of the ordinary such as a night shoot, the need to provide children with overnight accommodation or a change in agreed hours or location, the licensing authority must be consulted in advance.

The approved matron or someone else designated by the production must keep daily records which must be shown on demand to an inspector. The details required include:

- the date and location of performance/rehearsal;
- the times of arrival and departure;
- the hours of work and rest periods taken;
- the times of meals taken;
- the duration and subjects taught in tuition periods;
- details of any illnesses or accidents;
- dates of any medical examination of the child;
- dates of breaks in performance;

- details of the fees contracted and the persons to whom they are paid.

If it is intended to take any minors abroad to work, the relevant age is extended to include anyone under 18, and a special licence has to be obtained from:

 The Chief Magistrate
Bow Street
London WC2

All of this nightmarish regulation is of course to prevent the exploitation of children by monomaniac directors and producers, not to mention that most ferocious of predators, the Stage Mother.

The advice of the BBC to its production managers is 'Always adhere to the regulations, however great the pressure from the Director to go for another take. In working with children, every Director has to be aware that some compromise is often needed, and it is for you to ensure that the child's welfare is not sacrificed to artistic integrity.'

Directors of factual programmes will probably be able to avoid child actors, but problems of working with children can still occur. As a general point you may not use children, whether in a public or private place, even for simple vox pop interviews without proper parental permission and if the shoot involves any sort of directed activity there must be someone *in loco parentis* present such as a teacher, youth leader or doctor depending on the subject and the circumstances. Directorial requests must be made in consultation with them. On the other hand you have some latitude in using minors. You may for example use an amateur school or youth drama club production so long as the show is one which is of their own devising and your intentions are strictly documentary. Assuming parental permission and a contractual agreement with the organisers there will be no need to get involved with individual licensing (but watch out for copyright, Chapter 10).

Under no circumstances may anything be seen to interrupt the schooling of a child, so if possible any shooting involving minors should either be based around the school or take place during designated holidays.

Anyone in full-time education under the age of 18 will need the permission of a principal or head teacher as well as a parent in order to work on a production during term time.

Most documentary locations involving the young are likely to be in or around home or in an educational or similarly supervised environment. Many schools, particularly primary ones, will be happy to accept location crews particularly if the subject matter is educational or if the visit can be turned into an educational experience in itself.

Children and teachers alike are fond of seeing themselves on film or tape and the offer of a recording of the rushes or the final programme (assuming the footage has been included) will go a long way to winning friends. Both can be bitterly hurt to find that the promised tapes are forgotten, or that contrary to expectations they have been edited out of the transmission without prior explanation.

Schools will not be happy to disrupt any part of the teaching day for a television crew except insofar as the subject matter concerns teaching methods or the running of the school itself so requests for the turning off of bells or re-scheduling of break times will not go down well. If the subject matter is not educational, permission may be but restricted to lunch times and after school hours, in which case there may arise the problem of squaring the caretaker, cleaners or other ancillary staff.

If the intention is to use school premises as a location, the production will probably be told to shoot only during holiday periods and then to negotiate a facility fee. And if some of the pupils are to be involved, even for the odd day, there is still an obligation to ensure that teachers, parents or someone else in *loco parentis* is present.

Permission to use children during school time is normally given by the head teacher, but if the shooting involves school premises matters may get more complicated. Recent upheavals in the educational system may lead to confusion as to who permits whom for what. Most schools have been administered until recently by local education authorities, i.e. counties, county boroughs or metropolitan boroughs. Subsequently not only has there been a massive and complicated reorganisation of local government responsibilities but many schools have 'opted-out', or become self-governing but directly responsible to the Department of Education. Schools remaining under the control of the local education authorities will probably have to pass requests for shooting through a central press or public relations office, and time should be allowed for permission to be given. Schools which have opted-out will have greater administrative independence but applications may have to be submitted to a board of governors by the head teacher. In all cases time ought to be allocated to allow notification to be sent to parents. Parents who do not want their offspring to appear on camera have a perfect right to refuse permission. Opted-out schools, like privately owned establishments, are largely responsible for their own finances. The days of getting away with a free cassette or a small donation to the Swimming Pool Fund may be gone.

8

WORKING WITH ANIMALS

If animals do not complain as much as actors, there are plenty of people to complain on their behalf. Not all animals are equal. Once in front of a camera they are subject to fine legal distinctions.

Domestic animals

These should be the least problematical. However, the word of an owner about the docility of a pet needs to be taken with a pinch of salt. The sentence 'he's as soft as butter' is regularly followed by 'well he's never done that before.' Filming is as unnatural and disorientating an experience for animals as it is for humans and even trained sheep dogs can turn surly or neurotic. So any handling should be left strictly to the owner who should be present at all times. If animals are to be used all members of the crew and cast need to be warned. There are those who come out in a rash at the touch of cat hair or have a phobia about chickens.

Farm animals can raise problems especially at times of disease outbreaks and pigs may be subject to movement restrictions even when swine fever is not present in the country.

So long as pet animals are only required to do that for which they are trained, there should be no need for special precautions except to ensure through the owner that adequate shade, water and rest is provided for the animal's welfare. Domestic animals are covered by the Protection of Animals Act 1911 which makes it illegal to:

- ill treat, beat, infuriate, terrify or cause unnecessary suffering;
- transport in a way causing unnecessary suffering;
- cause, procure or assist in the baiting of any animal;
- administer drugs or poisons to any animal without reasonable excuse;
- cause any animal to be subjected to anything done without due care and humanity.

Investigative researchers and journalists should be mindful when getting involved with rustic pursuits such as badger baiting or cock fighting, which are, of course, illegal. However noble the motive, the investigator is likely to finish up in court as an accessory to a crime.

Performing animals

Any production involving extensive studio work or where an animal plays a significant dramatic role will need to hire a trained animal from one of the several specialist agencies. These animals will be familiar with the sort of environment they find themselves in and will be trained, so far as possible, to perform repeatedly a number of predictable acts. Performing animals are either domestic animals or captive bred wild ones. In the latter case it is the responsibility of the handler to give assurance that the animal has not come from the wild, particularly in the case of birds like parrots or birds of prey.

Performing animals are protected by the Performing Animals Regulation Act 1925 and it is up to an agency supplying animals to confirm that the training methods employed have been in compliance with the Act.

If animals are to be used extensively or over a long period in a studio or film set it is good practice to notify the Royal Society for the Prevention of Cruelty to Animals (RSPCA) which will designate an inspector to advise and be present to assist the production where appropriate.

It is sometimes proposed to use anaesthetics or tranquillisers on film animals. The Royal College of Veterinary Surgeons advises its members not to cooperate if this will be in any way:

- cruel or frightening;
- potentially dangerous to the well-being of the animal;
- achievable in some other way e.g. substituting another animal which is specifically trained for a trick, or using a dead or dummy animal substitute.

Performing animals are also subject to the Cinematograph Films Animals Act 1937 which makes it illegal to show any film which was directed or organised to inflict pain or terror or to cruelly goad any animal to fury. This raises the question of portraying in dramatic terms anything like a dog fight, whipping of a horse or heroic battles between man and beast. Obviously any such sequences have to be faked. It is essential to notify the RSPCA even if the director is quite confident that a brilliant use of camera angles and quick cutting will create the effect without any real distress being caused. Nothing is likely to upset the viewers more than a scene involving animal cruelty and the better the effect achieved, the more virulent the letters of complaint will be. Unless an animal welfare inspector is fully involved, prosecution may result regardless.

The internationalisation of broadcasting by satellite raises interesting questions of differing standards particularly throughout the EU. It is currently admissible to show footage of a bullfight in a documentary context but not if the producers deliberately set up the filming for their own express purposes. Whether it would be illegal to re-transmit a Spanish national channel which devotes long periods to bull fighting is less clear. Current EU regulations seem to allow governments to censor other members' television only in the interest of protecting minors.

Exotic animals

The Convention on the International Trade in Endangered Species (CITES) prohibits the import of a huge range of animals and animal products and a production employing more exotic creatures needs to be assured that they have been obtained legally.

A number of animals are scheduled under the Dangerous Wild Animals Act 1976 which is intended to prevent eccentric citizens using leopards as a fashion accessory or keeping cobras in the bath tub. The owner of a dangerous animal, an animal dealer or a zoo must hold a licence granted by the local government authority. It is essential before filming to ensure that the animal owner holds a valid licence and if there are doubts the local authority should be involved. If the animal concerned is used or accommodated in ways other than defined by the licence it can be confiscated or destroyed and costs recovered from the keeper. Old television hands have many a tale to tell of incontinent elephants, sex-crazed apes, monkeys in the lighting grid and pythons suddenly brought to hyperactivity under the lights. Always have enough handlers available to deal with the animals concerned and if in doubt ensure that a veterinary officer is present.

Animals in the wild

The documentary maker is not without problems of his or her own. Wild animals and plants in the UK are protected by the Wildlife and Countryside Act 1981. There is a schedule of pro-tected species to the Act but it is not exhaustive and it is wise to consider pretty well all birds, mammals and reptiles as protected unless they are clearly vermin or bred for game.

The filming of some animals and animal activities may involve acquiring a licence, nesting rare birds being a case in point. Natural history cameramen keep very close about their professional secrets but many of the most memorable sequences have been wholly or partly-constructed with studio set-ups or the use of trained or captive animals. Even some legitimately licensed activities such as the mist netting of migrating birds or live trapping of mammals inevitably risks some distress and a percentage of deaths. The use of live baits in fishing programmes can raise public protest and it is very much a matter for individual ethics in deciding how many times to return a fish to a net or keep it hooked for the sake of cutaway shots. If there is the suggestion that a production has caused distress to any animal there is a risk of prosecution.

The sensibilities of a section of the public have become increasingly acute and at the extreme fringe there are Animal Liberation activists capable of resorting to violence. This can be of concern to producers of scientific documentaries. Scientists working in fully licensed and supervised laboratories may become very unwilling to demonstrate their work, even if it involves no more than psychological testing or behavioural studies.

The first point of enquiry about any type of animal filming should be:

The Chief Veterinary Officer
Royal Society for the Prevention of Cruelty to Animals
Causeway
Horsham
Sussex RH12 1HG

Horses

The old cavalry definition of a horse is an animal which is dangerous at both ends and bloody uncomfortable in the middle. With this in mind horses should be treated with special attention during filming.

There are complex regulations and practical considerations involved in shooting charges, stampedes, runaway wagons, etc. which are beyond the scope of this book. A few simple rules should ensure the welfare of the animals:

- If there are going to be extensive re-takes, provide extra horses (one horse looks much the same as another if the colour is consistent).
- Only allow the horses to be used for production purposes.
- Causing a horse to fall by trips or pitfalls is illegal.
- Safety shoes must be fitted if the horse is to cross smooth floors or pavement, or else mats laid.
- Excessive use of reins or spurs must be avoided.
- Breakaway top rails must be used on jumps.
- Prop fence wire with rubber barbs only should be used.
- Front feet landing by rearing horses is compulsory.
- Provision must be made for all stock to be properly fed, watered and rested, and adequately corralled at night.

Looking after the horses is one thing and looking after the performers is another. The recent tragic death of the actor Roy Kinnear in a riding accident and the subsequent litigation is a reminder both of the perils of horse riding for the camera as well as the consequences of allowing the pressures of production to override safety considerations.

It is generally unwise to allow performers to perform any riding sequence more testing than sitting astride a placid and preferably static nag. It is doubly unwise to allow them to do so without a proper hard hat or ensuring that the animal is appropriately shod. Equity has conceded that proper horse masters and handlers as well as stunt artists and riding doubles need not be professional actors and with PACT has drawn up a code of practice including the following provisions:

- A shoot will engage an Equestrian Society approved horse master.
- The horse master may judge whether a performer is sufficiently skilled for a particular shot and will advise whether a skilled riding double should be employed or an alternative solution to the hazard be found.
- Where an artist has to ride, the horse master or Equestrian Society handler will be given adequate rehearsal time to judge the skill of the performer and advise accordingly.
- Details of proposed horse riding will be given at a pre-production meeting.
- There will be adequate production time given to any proposed action sequences and the time required agreed between the horse master, the performers and doubles or stunt artists, the producer and the director.

Documentary programme makers will also encounter horses. In a few parts of the world they are still sometimes a necessary means of transport, though the customary style of riding and horse care may be rather different to that advocated by an English riding club. Whether at a country race meeting or in the high Andes, the best advice is leave tacking, feeding and stabling to the experts and keep the camera at all times a clear 3 metres from either of the two dangerous ends.

9
PLAYING WITH FIRE

Stunts

If a shoot involves any activity that might be hazardous, a production ought seriously to consider engaging professional stunt artists. Under no circumstances should a director entertain the siren voices of amateurs, whether they are members of the team or untrained 'cowboys' longing to 'have a go before the camera'. A brilliant racing driver is not a stunt driver. A skilled rock climber is not to be trusted with enacting a struggle on the castle walls. Untrained stunt performers are likely to kill themselves and possibly other members of the cast, crew or public. Carelessly planned or executed stunts may result in the production insurance being void and a criminal prosecution under the Health and Safety at Work Act.

Stunts fall into two broad categories: those that may be performed by actors or presenters after proper expert advice and all safety precautions have been taken, and those which may be performed safely only by a trained stunt artist. Some actors and presenters take a macho attitude towards doing their own stunts. Wherever possible they should be discouraged. Admiration for great performers like Buster Keaton who did all his own stunts should be tempered by adding up the time Keaton must have spent off work waiting for his bones to mend.

The definition of stunt work in the BBC's safety rules sums up the situation.

> All stunts require meticulous and detailed planning. No stunt may be rehearsed or performed without the knowledge of a BBC Safety Adviser. No member of the public may participate in a stunt or be put at serious risk of injury by the performance of one. . . When artistes or contributors are involved in stunts an assessment of their fitness to do so must be made. In particular their age must be known where this is relevant. . . Competent specialists must be engaged to provide all necessary training.

> Such specialists must be satisfied that all participants have been adequately trained and are physically capable of performing a stunt before allowing it to proceed. The Producer must ensure that the specialist is fully briefed as to

what is required and is satisfied that the precautions are adequate to prevent injury to any of the participants or any person who may be affected by the performance of a stunt. The competent specialist referred to above must be present whenever the hazardous activity is being performed. Stunt Artistes, with indications or their areas of expertise are listed in Equity's Stunt Register. Whenever an artiste or contributor is to be 'flown' either an approved flying ballet contractor or a wireman under the direction of a stunt arranger must be engaged. . . Stunt artistes are responsible for taking measures to ensure their own safety, and the safety of those who may be affected by their activities, while they are performing the stunt specified in their contract. This responsibility extends to the selection of any equipment or materials to be used. The BBC is responsible for ensuring that any equipment it supplies is of the required quality.

It may be added that stunt artists are responsible for their personal insurance. Stunt men do not come cheap. There is a minimum Equity daily rate and extra payments may be due according to the complexity of the stunts arranged.

The register of stunt artists is held by Equity. This is because stunt artists are first and foremost actors. Their job is not to directly court danger but to give the appearance of doing so. They are highly experienced in the use of lenses and camera angles and will advise the director on means to 'cheat' and on moves to heighten the impression of danger and suspense. They are trained in the art of illusion, not in the business of taking unnecessary risks. It might appear much cheaper to sign up professional athletes but that would be to miss the point. A stunt artist is an actor who has some specific skills. An athlete is simply a sportsman and the chances of turning one into a competent actor overnight are remote.

Moreover a principal job of stuntmen is to appear as stunt doubles and this involves the dramatic skill to imitate another performer. So only those who already have full membership of Equity will be considered for the Stunt Register. Recruits must be between 18 and 30 years old and be able to provide medical certificates and a certificate of competence in first aid. There is a professional hierarchy:

- *Probationary members*: may only work under the full-time supervision of a full member of the Register for a minimum period of three years.
- *Intermediate members*: may arrange and perform his or her own stunts but not those involving any other performers or stunt artists.

- *Full members*: are promoted after a minimum of two years as an intermediate member and are qualified to design and arrange stunts involving other performers or a team of stunt artists.

All stunt artists must hold a portfolio of a minimum of six special skills certificated by relevant organisations. These range from the martial arts, fencing and boxing to stunt driving, trampolining, mountaineering and scuba diving. Stunt performers' reputations are circulated very much by word of mouth. Many of the more experienced become specialist fight arrangers or second unit directors for action sequences.

A word of caution
Many actors and actresses advertise in Equity their special skills such as fencing and riding. Walk-ons similarly are enthusiastic to qualify for the extra payments that come with special skills. If these involve anything more risky than ballroom dancing, a qualified stunt arranger should be involved.

Arms and armourers

Anything capable of launching a projectile from a peashooter to a grenade launcher must be treated as a lethal weapon whether loaded or not. So must any knife, sword or bludgeon entrusted to the hands of a performer even if it is an imitation or theatrical property.

When staging fights, there will be probably be a need to engage a fight arranger or stunt doubles. If real or blank firing weapons are used the production will almost certainly require a qualified armourer who holds the appropriate licences. There are several categories of gun licence:

- The *black powder licence* enables the bearer to handle muzzle loading weapons. Black powder licences are often held by special effects designers and members of historic battle societies. Powder and wadding are dangerous and disfiguring at close range; primed duelling pistols and the like should always be kept under the close supervision of the armourer.
- The *shotgun licence* may be obtained from the local police and is the one commonly held by farmers and sportsmen. Police will need to check the bona fides of applicants and assure themselves about the security of the arms and

ammunition. The possession of a sawn-off shotgun, even a replica, is a serious criminal offence and must never be seen on any public location.

- A *firearms certificate* is necessary for owning any modern rifled weapon and hand gun. It is obtained with great difficulty and subject to stringent conditions. It is normally restricted to members of recognised gun clubs and those with demonstrable needs such as gun dealers, deer farmers, veterinary officers and the like.

- The *Home Office Section Five Permit* enables the holder to use weapons capable of continuous automatic fire. Very few weapons dealers even have a permit and fully automatic weapons have been withdrawn from most gun clubs. If a production needs automatic weapons it will be necessary to confirm that there is a supplier with the required permit. Since the tragic massacres at Hungerford and Dunblane, access to handguns and semi-automatic weapons has become increasingly restricted and a total ban on them has been proposed.

- Authority to handle the full range of weapons is embodied in the Home Office certificate of 'Registered Firearms Dealership'. The main suppliers of weapons for theatrical use and broadcast television companies employing armourers should be RFD holders.

The only weapons which do not need specific licences are low-velocity air guns, blocked blank firing starting pistols and antique weapons used exclusively as ornaments. De-activated military weapons like replicas are easily purchased without a licence being required though there is police concern that some of these might be restored to working order. Replicas have been increasingly used in robberies and may become controlled. The latest major legislation was the Firearms Act 1968 but if the production has any doubts, enquiries should be addressed to the Crime Prevention Officer of the nearest police station.

Fully practical weapons must be supervised by an armourer who will be responsible for the secure transport of arms and ammunition and their safety on set. Weapons will always be kept securely locked between times of use. Blank firing weapons can be very dangerous and almost annually there are accidents caused by mishandled weapons or weapons wrongly assumed to be unloaded. Metal cased blanks should never be used with an open ended gun or automatic weapon with a restrictor sleeve as fragments of brass can blind or maim. Even powder grains or bits of wadding are dangerous. The British Armed Forces recommend a minimum safe distance of 30 metres where blank ammunition is being fired.

Actors have to be properly instructed by the armourer during rehearsal how to handle a particular weapon and above all shown how to 'aim off' and still look convincing when pointing the weapon towards anyone else.

Weapons and ammunition should be issued and checked back between takes and in the event of any going astray it is the job of the production manager to call a halt to the filming and to conduct a full search with everyone present. Replicas should be treated with the same respect as operational weapons.

Firearms are not the only weapons to require the assistance of an armourer. Bows and arrows or slingshots are potentially lethal. Crossbows should be treated as though they were rifles. Edged weapons, if not supplied purely as costume accessories, may have to be hired from an armourer and supervised whilst in use. Even in a properly choreographed fight sequence, buttons can come off fencing foils or too energetically clashed blunted swords can turn into sharp saw edges. The armourer will probably bring a grindstone to remedy such an event.

Under the Criminal Justice Act certain categories of weapon are illegal to import or to carry. These include flick knives, knuckle dusters, sword sticks, a number of bizarre oriental martial arts weapons such as 'death stars' and lately canisters of CS gas. Anything that gets fashionable in criminal circles fairly swiftly gets added to the list. In a stage production of *West Side Story* it is simple to get away with plastic fake switch blades. In close-up on the small screen the real article might be required. Prohibited weapons should not be used on location and an armourer should be consulted about their supply or use on a set.

Using arms on location requires the usual practical application of common sense:

- If real or replica guns are to be used, the police must be warned.
- Uncased weapons may not be carried in public places. Even an air rifle must have a carrying case if carried on or adjacent to a public highway.
- Never stage a fight or shoot out where an unwary public might be alarmed and summon the police (see pp. 3–5).
- If explosions or sustained firing are needed the best location will be a firing range or quarry under proper local supervision.

There are several additional reasons for going to a professional armourer. Although antique and replica weapons can be obtained easily from collectors and dealers for a modest hire fee they will expect them returned in the condition in which they left, unlikely if they have featured in an energetic fight routine.

Weapons supplied by the armourer may come with accoutrements like scabbards, sword belts, holsters, etc. These might also be part of a suggested wardrobe ordered from the costumiers. There is no point in paying twice.

Armourers may also be able to provide convincing rubber or foam replicas. These are particularly useful for replicating military weapons which are very expensive to hire. They also ensure that the actors are less likely to knock out each others' teeth.

The cost of hiring weapons is extremely variable and depends on the scarcity of the model required and its availability in stock. Some commonly requested items such as Lee Enfield rifles or Luger pistols might be cheap and hire charges may be calculated at about 15 per cent of the replacement value per week. Some armourers will hold private stocks of weapons but many will only undertake to search around other suppliers for specific items. It may pay to shop around yourself.

If the main reference directories cannot provide the name of an armourer convenient for the chosen location you can look through the telephone trade directory for arms dealers and enquire if they have television experience. An enquiry at the local television station might get a recommendation for someone suitable. The largest, but not the only, supplier in London is probably:

Bapty's
703 Harrow Road
London N10 5NY

Documentary makers, unless making dramatised reconstructions, will normally be working with either the armed forces and police or else properly supervised gun clubs and ranges which have safety as a priority. The subject matter might, however, encompass anything from armed insurgents to deer poachers or Western quick-draw enthusiasts. Amongst the commonsense tips are:

- Keep everyone behind the gun barrels (pretty obvious but not always conducive to getting the best shots).
- When shooting close alongside an automatic weapon do note how and which side it ejects to avoid getting an earful of hot cartridge case.
- In any confined range or where there is sustained firing supply every one with ear defenders.
- Wherever possible do a detailed recce or get the participants to give a complete demonstration before asking the cameraman and recordist to take positions.

- Watch out for the member of the team (usually male) for whom weapons have a possibly fatal attraction. Maintain a strict 'hands off' discipline.
- If a blank firing weapon is to be fired towards the camera a sheet of toughened glass or plastic, preferably supplied by an armourer, should be placed well in front of the lens.

Special effects

'Special effects' conjure up images of exploding bombs and burning buildings.

Although the spectacular bangs and crashes are part of the special effects designer's trade there are a host of routine effects regularly needed by productions as diverse as comedy, scientific, educational and children's programmes.

Model making is a very significant part of the effects designer's work. The creation of prostheses to alter the features of a performer is often the work of special effects in cooperation with the make-up supervisor. Breakaway furniture and safely shattering glassware and windowpanes are constructed or supplied by special effects.

A lot of these, like simple and harmless rain, frost and smoke effects can be tried on a DIY basis without needing special effects personnel, assuming you have a stage manager or floor manager willing and able. Smoke guns and dry ice machines can be hired from special effects companies on a self-operating basis, although PACT recommends the use of trained operatives.

Anything involving flames, floods, bullet hits or pyrotechnics will definitely require the input of specialists.

The most spectacular of special effects are often employed in conjunction with stunt performers. They are meant to look dangerous and when improperly supervised probably are. So this is another area where the enthusiastic amateur should be held at arms' length. Into this category must be placed many types of speciality variety performers, circus acts and so on who may be quite accustomed to leaping through hoops of fire in their own environments, but without the closest of supervision can be a menace in the quite different conditions of a television studio or location shoot.

Traditionally special effects designers have come into the television industry from a wide range of craft and professional backgrounds and the reputations of individuals and companies gets around very much by word of mouth. Companies advertise in the trade press and directories like *The Knowledge* and normally will have show reels of their past successes. Alternatively a director might see a set of attractive effects on transmission and trace the designer responsible through the closing credits.

Special effects are not just for the 'big boys' to play with. A good designer will be willing to advise on many economical ways to achieve the desired results.

A storm might involve two fire tenders and remotely operated rain heads mounted on cherry-picker cranes. A similar effect might be achieved by closer shooting and a simple mechanism connected to a garden hose pipe. Film and television are all about illusion and many a production has come to grief because a director has forgotten this basic fact and gone overboard on design and special effects.

Every effect, with or without stunt performers, ought to be completely safe. Stunt performers and cameramen or women will often have a long working relationship with certain effects companies and may give recommendations. Some cameramen on the other hand suspect special effects designers collectively as homicidal pyromaniacs and when given a safe operating distance prefer to double it and then add 10 metres.

There is a register of approved special effects designers drawn up by PACT in collaboration with BECTU. But the register is not exhaustive and there are many excellent specialists in areas such as pyrotechnics or model making who do not belong. BECTU has tried to establish a series of grades and qualifications similar to those applicable to stunt performers set by Equity. A designer following this path would spend five years as a trainee, and five years as a technician working as part of a team before graduating to senior technician and then waiting yet five years longer to become a special effects supervisor qualified to design and supervise the most difficult work. At this level the effects designer is in name or substance a second unit director.

The breathtaking advances in production and post-production techniques is creating new demands on effects designers aeons away from the whizz-bang-crash traditional technology. The world of virtual reality sets and digital video effects combining live action, model stage work, puppetry and animated art work means that very great numbers of television commercials, trailers, programme junctions and logos depend on a special effects design input. Advances in puppetry have brought about the high-tech concept of animatronics. The infinite variety of circumstances make it difficult to draw up any comprehensive list of guidelines for working with special effects. However, there are some basic principles.

- Work out the effects requirements as far ahead as possible. Apart from a few standard prop items there will probably be construction time involved.

- Make sure the effects designer and set designer work hand in glove from the beginning and have the effects designer at every location recce.
- Keep a close eye on the budget. This is the area where quite literally the question 'how many bangs for the bucks?' applies. Wherever possible rehearse effects and pre-record difficult ones separately.
- Both special effects and stunt work can take time and may not work at first take. Leave plenty to time in the schedule for re-setting.
- If there is any real risk ensure that qualified first aid assistance is on hand and fire fighting equipment or support is sufficient.
- Even if the shoot is on private property but there will be noticeable smoke, flames or explosions, make sure to warn the local fire brigade and police.
- Both special effects and stunt work can be time consuming and tiring. Wherever possible schedule them at the early part of the shooting day. The risk of accidents increases as personnel become weary and the director is tempted to try to get the notorious 'just one final take' in the can.

Insurance

As this book is dedicated to the proposition that if anything can go wrong it will, the question of insurance arises.

Full-time employees of major companies will be insured according to the obligatory employers' liability and local agreement with their trade unions. There also may be voluntary contributory schemes for insurance against death or injury, but company insurance cover might not extend to the loss of personal goods, for example property lost or destroyed during air travel or stolen on location. The degree of cover where it applies may not be generous.

Since an increasingly large majority of workers in film and television are now self-employed or employed by small companies the question of personal insurance needs attention. For example the use of private cars is often necessary yet a private motor insurance policy may specifically exclude the use of a vehicle for work purposes or the transportation of work personnel. The obliging production manager who gives a lift to the hotel to a star performer and then has an accident involving injury to that performer might have a hard time with his insurance company.

Broadcasters and television workers are regarded as risky propositions by insurance companies and often face high premiums. There are brokers specialising in the insurance of film and television productions, and any contract negotiated between a producer and a client or commissioning body ought to take account of the insurance implications. For the absolute minimum cover this should be calculated at 1 per cent of the gross budget but for insurance against all eventualities this could rise to over 3 per cent.

Whether the production involvement is a major feature film or a commissioned wedding video the insurance cover must be appropriate. At one end of the scale the nervous breakdown of a movie star might destroy a film, but at the other an exploding lamp or carelessly placed cable can have consequences just as grave proportionately. Insurance cover comes at several levels, as described in the following sections.

Employers' liability

Obligatory under the Employers Liability Compulsory Insurance Act 1969. It is for unlimited liability covering death, injury or illness at the place of work for anyone whether salaried, freelance or in any way connected professionally with a production. For a claim to succeed negligence must be shown. It should be recalled though that under the Health and Safety at Work Act this does not mean that all negligence can be left to an insurance claim as it will likely result in the criminal prosecution of the guilty parties.

Public liability

Although not a statutory obligation every commercial undertaking will normally take out a public liability insurance, the normal minimum cover usually quoted being £1 million. Liability should cover property as well as third parties and many location proprietors will wisely not allow a production on the premises without evidence of valid public liability cover. The standard indemnity may not cover vehicles, private or hired, used during a production and cover may have to be specifically extended.

Negative insurance

This cover is appropriate to shoots scheduled over a period and involving contracted artists or locations. It covers the costs of a re-shoot brought about by mechanical breakdown, faulty film stock or force majeur.

Errors and omissions

Particularly appropriate to companies involved in factual programming errors and omissions insurance covers against civil damages for libel, copyright infringement and trespass.

All risk equipment and properties

Companies which own their own technical equipment have to weigh up the advantages of paying for fully comprehensive cover. Insurance against fire and theft on a studio premises can be expensive but cover against loss or damage on locations can be so costly that many companies will choose to risk only a minimal coverage.

Most companies do, however, hire equipment. This will mean that the company will be responsible for the insurance of all items on hire from the moment of collection. This may be arranged by the rental company but for most goods will be the responsibility of the hirer.

The rental terms can repay study before a decision to take insurance risks is made. For example costume hire can attract stiff penalties if there is staining, tearing or missing buttons on return. Even modest damage to hired properties or costumes can result in a full replacement charge.

Union insurance

There are special obligatory terms for insurance agreed between PACT and the main television companies with the broadcast unions to cover special circumstances. These include working in dangerous conditions (in the air, up mountains, at sea or with stunt performers) and overseas. Personnel may refuse to work without evidence of such insurance cover.

The minimum capital sum insured for overseas locations in 1995 was £50 000 and the medical and emergency travel expenses cover £250 000.

It is possible to insure against anything, of course, if you can find someone to take your bet and can afford the premium. Amongst the items frequently insured against by film companies are:

- the weather;
- unreliability of star performers;
- underwater filming;
- aircraft;
- hijack, ransom and political upheaval.

It pays to discuss the many options with a specialist insurance broker.

10

COPYRIGHT

Copyright is the body of law which protects the authors and owners of original works from the unlicensed piracy of their labours by others. The first principle is 'If it's worth copying, it's worth protecting.'

There are two broad categories of copyright – original and secondary. Original copyright protects the rights of the creators of work such as writers, artists, composers and even computer programmers. Secondary rights protect those who have made a financial investment in the original work such as publishers, recording, broadcast and software companies.

So almost any original work is likely to be subject to at least two copyrights. In reality the use of any work in a television context is likely to turn out more complicated than that. A simple piece of music may well involve separate copyrights in the composition, the lyrics, the performers, the music publishers, the arrangers and the recording company. A quite unexceptional television programme might involve copyright in a registered format, live performances, commissioned music, recorded music, still photographs, original graphics, literary quotations, archive film or video clips and more besides. Each of these elements might in turn involve a complex of separate rights. The final programme will naturally attract its own copyright.

The nightmarish complexity of television and film copyright is due to the nature of the beast. Film and television are collaborative creative exercises. Almost every creative participant is at some time an author and at some point an exploiter of the copyright of others.

The financing of productions and the marketing of them may involve third-party negotiated secondary sales fees and distribution by tape, disk, cable, satellite or computer as well as domestic and overseas broadcast co-producers all of whom will demand copyright clearance.

Copyright is so wide ranging that nobody can claim to know it all, and it is the domain of some very specialised legal firms. But if copyright is a pain for almost everyone except the lawyers it is also the bedrock on which the whole network of fees, commissions and contracts in our business is based. Without a workable copyright payment system, the television industry could not exist.

There is no copyright in facts. Some things are not subject to copyright:

- There is no copyright in information. Two current affairs programmes might give approximately the same reports using approximately the same words and using much the same images but unless one has substantially quoted the precise script of the other or copied the actual footage there is no breach of copyright.

- There is no copyright in events. In 1991 the BBC took the satellite service BSB to court for using some of its broadcast footage of World Cup football in its own news reports. The material used was limited to the main goals scored and the source was acknowledged on screen. The court ruled that there was no copyright in a football match and the limited use of footage was 'fair dealing'.

- Copyright material may be copied for criticism. Any kind of copyright work including films and photographs may be reproduced for the purposes of criticism or review so long as the quotations used are brief and to the point, and the source is fully acknowledged at the time. Any attempt to use whole scenes under the pretext of criticism, or show a series of still photographs in a documentary feature with a critical content would be challenged in the courts. In practice most productions, like new TV drama series, feature films and pop videos, provide selected clips to reviewers prior to distribution or broadcast in the interests of publicity.

- There is no copyright in ideas. It is the constant worry of factual programme makers that they might have their projects rejected by a commissioning editor only to see an identical work produced later by another hand. The independent producer or writer is particularly vulnerable as original programme ideas are a form of 'intellectual capital' unprotected until given some material expression.

On this last point there is some possibility of getting copyright protection for written programme treatments or formats but only if these are sufficiently original and detailed. The recourse is to register these with a third party. Both PACT and the Writers' Guild offer a registration service to their members. Alternatively the author can send the written material by registered post either to a third party such as a lawyer or bank, or to a home address leaving the postmarked envelope unopened. Another solution is to deposit the original work with the Copyright Register at Stationers' Hall in London. A fee of £30 ensures registration for a period of seven years with the possibility of renewal thereafter for an extra fee. The address is:

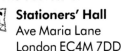

Stationers' Hall
Ave Maria Lane
London EC4M 7DD

Registering a format or script does not ensure copyright. A 1989 Privy Council ruling denied the existence of copyright in game-show formats, when it ruled against Hughie Green, creator of 'Opportunity Knocks', who tried to sue the New Zealand Broadcasting Corporation for copying his format. The decision that even blatant copying is not protected by law has caused concern. Because of this the Patent Office has issued two consultative documents, the latest in 1996, proposing to give legal status to the concept of 'intellectual property' and extend copyright protection to any 'sufficiently elaborated scheme or plan for a series of programmes'.

There is an alternative means for defending an idea. In 1981 an independent writer successfully sued Thames Television for breach of confidence on the grounds that he had discussed with them his ideas for a musical series which they had then gone on to make as 'The Rock Follies' without employing him. The only sure way to ensure the confidentiality of ideas though is to enter into a written correspondence, keep agreed signed minutes, or ask for a 'consideration' or purely nominal fee for the work. At this point a legal contract will exist, although trying to enforce it later may be mightily expensive.

The law

Copyright has been defined by successive acts, the Copyright Act 1911, the Copyright Act 1956 and the Copyright, Designs and Patents Act 1988. Copyright protection is about to be further complicated by the imminent harmonisation of UK and EU laws. Under the 1988 Act the duration of protection is as follows:

- *Films and broadcasts.* Fifty years from the end of the calendar year of the first showing or transmission. There have been cases where people have jumped the gun and started to use material from the actual anniversary date of expiry as opposed to the impending New Year; and paid a heavy penalty as a result.
- *Literary, dramatic, musical or artistic work.* Fifty years from the death of the author. But under the 1956 Act works published for the first time after the death of the author are

copyright from the date of publication. This can be a headache for a researcher on a historical series. A 200 year old diary might have been first published only in recent times and therefore be subject to a new copyright.

A major spanner has been thrown into the works by EU harmonisation which will entail all member states adopting the German copyright rule of protection for 70 years. Authors like Kipling, Galswothy and James Joyce are suddenly going to come back into copyright.

At the time of writing Westminster has still not ratified the new law and it seems likely that work already commissioned or begun before the ratification takes effect will still be subject to the old 50 year rules. Anyone wanting to use material from George Orwell or Conan Doyle had better join the rush before their estates are re-activated.

Who owns copyright?

Copyright is intellectual property so like any other kind of property it can be sold, assigned, licensed, leased or bequeathed. A copyright owner has the sole legal right to authorise the use of the work for any purpose whatsoever, and has the 'negative' right to go to law to prevent any unauthorised use.

Copyright in films (in law any medium recording moving images is described as film) under the 1988 Act is owned by the person who makes the arrangements necessary for the making of the film or recording. This would normally be the production company. Live broadcasts belong to the person making the broadcast, formerly the BBC or IBA but now extended to cable and other broadcast media. Copyright does not belong to the person who foots the bill, anymore than someone who buys a painting does not automatically buy the copyright to the work, only the object.

This has implications for even small productions. A company which commissions a television commercial or promotional video does not automatically own the copyright unless the production company or agency has specifically assigned it. The commissioning company cannot make free with the material in another context without coming to an agreement with the production company and any performers originally contracted. Corporate clients who switch agencies and producers can find it difficult to comprehend that their own advertising commercials may no longer belong to them. Copyright in the programme does not necessarily bring with it all the contributory copyrights. So the scene is set for the production company to try to clear 'all rights' from each contributor and for each contributor to cling on to his or her individual rights except in lieu of a generous payment. Much depends on the circumstances. There is probably not a lot of point in fighting for rights in a corporate video since the footage will probably have a very limited shelf life. Conversely, a broadcast drama series will probably be intended for a long history of repeats, adaptations and distribution through various media, and contributors will need to negotiate contracts with extreme care if they are not to sign away their dues.

The Copyright Act simply states who does own copyright in a simple case, not who ought to hold copyright. So to avoid conflict any change in ownership must be put clearly in writing. Production companies commissioned either by corporate clients or broadcast companies are normally expected to take contractual responsibility for all copyright clearances before handing over the finished work.

The commonest ways that copyright is transferred are:

- *Assignment*: a contributor or agency assigns either all copyright or a modified copyright to someone else. This must be done formally in writing and is very often a necessary part of the initial contract of engagement. For example a performer may assign copyright for the exploitation of work in an original context, e.g. a training video, but not for alternative exploitation such as broadcast, overseas sales or reuse in subsequent productions.

- *Licence*: when productions are spoken of as 'sold' to a television company it would be more accurate to talk of them being licensed. Licence gives the purchaser limited rights, normally exclusive ones, to copy, distribute, or exploit work over a stated period.

- *Consent*: it is accepted that in broadcast terms anyone willingly appearing in front of a camera for an interview or statement has given consent for its use and thereby waived copyright in their performance. Public speeches or remarks count as events over which there is no copyright, so an indiscreet politician or company director cannot try to invoke copyright to prevent the broadcast of an embarrassing public gaffe. Otherwise it is advisable to get a simple release form signed as an interviewee can have second thoughts about appearing in a programme and legitimately withdraw permission at the last moment.

It is worth noting that all material including unused rushes, out takes, atmosphere tracks and so on remain in copyright. The production company may wish to retain these for later use as stock shots. The commissioning agency may want these for reasons of commercial confidentiality or use in subsequent productions. Who holds these and who remains responsible for clearances ought to be agreed and put in writing.

Moral rights

The 1988 Act brought into being in English law the concept of 'moral rights' or 'rights of paternity' in copyright. The concept is a novel one here but is well precedented in Europe and the harmonisation of laws may bring moral rights into prominence here. Moral rights belong to individuals and some of them exist automatically unless expressly waived as a part of a contract of engagement. They tend to appear vague and most of them have yet to be tested in British Courts:

The right to be identified

Writers, directors and composers have the right to be publicly credited on the credits or pages of a script or score. This right does not come automatically. To confirm it, the person has to write formally to the producer or copyright owning company asserting the moral right to a credit and establishing in what form the billing will be made.

The right to prevent derogatory treatment

This is the right of writers and directors not to have their works mutilated or so altered as to reflect adversely on their professional reputations. Defining this will be appallingly difficult as wounded egos are part and parcel of the industry. More than one director or writer has walked off a production or withdrawn a name from the credits in protest at work being re-edited or shortened. Moral rights have been invoked in France in an attempt to prevent the interruption of televised feature films by advertisements. In the United States there has been similar protest about the digital colouring of black and white originals. (As one wag put it 'you can't take Casablanca seriously when you find out that Humphrey Bogart wore a brown suit.') The use of original footage for satirical purposes or inclusion in an unforeseen context such as an advertisement might infringe moral rights. The plaintiff in any case will have to demonstrate more than affronted pride when seeking damages. It is not likely that this moral right will extend to preventing an executive producer demanding a complete re-cut of a documentary or a news editor ruthlessly cropping a beautifully composed photograph.

Standard PACT contracts for directors propose that moral rights should be waived. However, cases where pictures and commentary have been edited to alter the original intentions of the director have been observed. The Directors' Guild is currently taking up the issues on the grounds that a producer or broadcaster retains the right to edit any commissioned work but may not do so to the detriment of the professional integrity of the director. Such moral rights may soon result in a test case.

The right against false attribution
The right to have a name removed from credits or from having original authorship falsely attributed, most likely when an adaptation or re-make trades heavily on the name of an original author or where re-writes have made the original work of a screenwriter unrecognisable.

The right of commissioners of private work
The right of those who have commissioned private photographs, films or videos to prevent them being shown in public. There are alternative means to veto the indiscreet use of private material by invoking confidentiality laws.

Incidental use
Because every original work is subject to copyright – paintings, prints, trade names, typefaces, advertisements and even in some contexts public buildings – it would be a nightmare for any director to try to clear every single appearance of copyright material. Designers would have to create sets of complete fantasy if every textile design or bottle of ketchup had to be specifically non-identifiable.

It is allowable for the use of copyright material to be used 'incidentally' in a programme. What this means precisely is somewhat vague and depends on the circumstances. For example, the set of a youth programme may be incidentally decorated with copyright protected posters, but if one piece of artwork played a significant role its appearance would be judged in no way incidental. If in doubt stick to a print of 'The Monarch of the Glen' and check that Sir Edwin Landseer has been dead for 70 years first.

Remedies
There are going to be times when attributing copyright becomes almost impossible. The older the material the more likely it is that this is going to arise. Damages for a breach of the law are not likely to be excessive so long as it is made clear that every

reasonable effort has been made to establish if copyright exists. Authors die, or emigrate, or write under pseudonyms. Publishers and production companies go out of business and records are lost. Unattributed footage emerges from the back of forgotten film vaults or private attics.

In such circumstances the intending user may decide to take a calculated risk of contravening the law. In the comparatively straightforward area of print publishing you may be covered if after suitable enquiries you take space in a reputed journal like *The Times Literary Supplement* stating that all investigations have been fruitless and that you intend to publish none the less. Such a declaration should also appear as part of the published work. The author might still emerge from the woodwork. The worst scenario is that he or she emerges immediately before publication and obstinately refuses consent. It is more likely though that the author would emerge after publication.

In this case recompense should be offered commensurate with what would be normally be regarded as the current rate for the job. If exorbitant claims are made the defendant can turn to a professional body, such as the Society of Authors' to ask for confirmation of a reasonable fee. And if even then you find yourself in court it is very unlikely that the judge would award more than an estimated loss of earnings. As with most legal matters the cost is not in the penalty but in going to court in the first place.

This is a very different matter from deliberately trying to dodge copyright obligations or, worse still, deliberately going against the wishes of the copyright holder. Under these circumstances the courts will take a very dim view of your actions and damages may be substantial. What may be worse in commercial terms is a court injunction preventing broadcast or publication. A demand for the 'handing up' of copies contravening copyright is one redress for an aggrieved copyright owner. In 1995 a well-promoted pop music album had to be withdrawn on the second day of sale because the copyright holder of a single sound-effect track which had been 'sampled' from a previous recording would not accept a proposed fee.

Establishing copyright

The courts will not act in copyright cases without proof of authorship or ownership. The easiest and most useful way for a producer or writer to make this clear is to incorporate the © copyright symbol with the date and his or her name at the beginning and/or the end of a recorded programme, and for a writer to do likewise with a script or screenplay. (Some authors program their PCs to add this routinely to pages.)

The copyright symbol has no legal force in itself. Sticking your name and a symbol on the end of your work does not automatically protect you. But any breach of your copyright subsequently can be shown to have been done wilfully.

Criminal law

Almost, but not all, copyright disputes are matters of civil law. Deliberate copying, importation or sale of copyright material can attract criminal penalties which may involve up to two years imprisonment or an unlimited fine on indictment after trial, or two months imprisonment with a £2000 fine from a magistrates court.

The law was aimed at the makers of pirate videotapes and sound recordings. This illegal trade is international and there are established links with more sinister forms of organised crime and pornography.

But criminal abuse of copyright has occurred in far more respectable company. The Reliance Mutual Insurance Company way brought to the High Court by two film production companies for unauthorised copying of management training videos. This followed a court order authorising a search of two offices of the Insurance Company which revealed 125 illegal copies and resulted in a fine of £150 000 plus substantial costs.

The threat to educational and training productions is proportionately as great as to feature films. Training tapes have a long shelf life and are often produced on shoestring budgets with minimum numbers of projected sales in mind. The organisations they serve may not be fully aware of their copyright obligations. More likely they try to cut costs on the basis that discovery of unlicensed copying is unlikely and the producers are too insignificant to afford legal action. To fight such cases there is a professional organisation which offers legal support to aggrieved productions.

 The Training Media Copyright Association
Bolster House
5/6 Clipstone Street
London W1P 7EB

Most of the professional associations such as Equity, PACT and IVCA will offer expert advice on copyright matters as well as propose model forms of contract, waivers, licences and so on as appropriate to their members. Screenwriters are advised to join the Writers' Guild which like Equity and the Musicians' Union, has negotiated detailed copyright agreements with both PACT and the major Broadcasting Companies.

 The Writers' Guild of Great Britain
430 Edgware Road
London W2 1EH

and advice for writers is also available from:

The Society of Authors
Broadcasting Committee
84 Drayton Gardens
London SW10 9SB

Most of the professional associations and collecting societies publish explanatory and advisory material about copyright as it affects their members,

The main reference book for the 1988 Act is *Blackstone's Guide to the Copyright, Designs and Patents Act 1988*. This contains a very readable commentary as well as the complete text of the law.

But now for something completely different
At the end of 1995 the copyright situation is in a greater than usual state of confusion.

The Department of Trade and Industry has published a Rental and Lending Rights Directive and a Term Copyright Directive, which came fully into force on 1 January 1996. The Directives bring UK and EU laws into line and apart from extending most copyright terms to 70 years include directions on remuneration, databases, cable and satellite, and rental. At the same time the EU has published a Green Paper called Copyright and Neighbouring Rights in the context of the Information Society, which in course will result in further changes in the implementation of copyright laws.

In short the explosion of information technology has enormous implications for copyright. At its simplest the spread of satellite and cable channels may bring dozens, and very likely hundreds, of television channels into the home by the end of this decade. Policing copyright in this international cat's cradle of programming is the challenge facing the various collection societies. Equity has just set up a collection society, PAMRA, similar to those in the music industry to collect and distribute fees to its members. The pressure by production and transmission companies to demand the assignment of all rights by authors and performers will increase, as will the determination of the latter not to sign away their future incomes. Early shots have been fired by an alliance of the main professional associations at BBC radio. The BBC has demanded that independent productions be delivered free of all copyright in perpetuity. Actors, writers and musicians are not amused.

Of more importance is the rise of the Information Superhighway. The starry-eyed enthusiasts of cyberspace foresee a world in which all information is freely and instantaneously available to all at the tap of a keyboard. As fibre optic cables become standard and computer technology improves the highest quality sounds and pictures may be transmitted and received. Unfortunately the implication could be the destruction of the idea of copyright or at least the practical means to enforce it.

Legislation has been proposed in the USA which would make the administrators of computer networks responsible for copyright. At the moment in the USA they are classified as common carriers like the Post Office and not as publishers. Such suggestions are opposed by the network administrators as being impossible to police, and by those who believe that the Superhighway is the ultimate in freedom of information. Under the proposed new rules networks would be liable for any copyright material stored on any of the machines of their millions of clients. There exist, or are envisaged, encryption techniques to prevent computer transmitted material being copied or registering when copyright material is accessed. The proposed rules would make it an offence to tamper with any of these, which should throw down the gauntlet to amateur hackers worldwide. Apart from the costs and technological complexities involved any legal restriction could have repercussions for libraries and other freely available sources of reference.

Now read on ...

Film copyright

Documentary directors in particular very frequently need to use news footage, archive film and videotape and even extracts from feature films. Under the Copyright Act news film is put into the same category as newspaper photographs. It is covered for 50 years from the date of publication. The ownership of the copyright will depend on the status of the photographer. If the film has been shot by a staff employee or a freelance under contract the rights belong to the production company. If the footage originated with a freelance photographer or amateur video maker, copyright belongs to the film maker. Moral rights also apply.

Feature films are further covered as dramatic works and are protected for 50 years from the death of the author. Thus we come back to the question of who is the author of a collective enterprise such as a film? The copyright ramifications of feature films are particularly bedevilled because of their international status from the very outset. Films are not even made without complex deals between backers to deal with distribution and marketing rights, and in most instances anyone wanting access to material has to beware of American copyright implications as well as European ones. If you have ever wondered why the end credits on US films often seem half as long as the rest of the movie this is the reason. In films shot since 1960 practically all of them are entitled to some kind of copyright fee unless they have contractually signed away their rights.

Even old material is not without its complications. In the USA a film becomes 'public domain' after 50 years of a first showing. But the copyright of authors and artists may persist. The British Film Institute considers that no copyright in a film can be regarded as totally clear until every last screen writer and stunt man is safely in the grave. Even then in some circumstances copyright can be extended. It would be an unwise director who allowed so much as a glimpse of Mickey Mouse on a television screen in the background of a set, even though the famous mouse is 70 years old.

The only pictures guaranteed to be free are those released about the time of distribution for review or publicity purposes. Even then the exemption can prove temporary. Both publicity clips and still photographs of long past films can still attract copyright permission for their subsequent use.

There are separate copyrights in the pictures and in the sound track which raises the additional problem of music. Under the American Copyright regulations of 1960, the Directors Guild of America collects payment for every extract from a film started after that date, the rate being set according to the length of the extract shown, starting with clips of under 30 seconds. The Writers' Guild of America operates much the same system for screen writers. It is up to the producer wanting to use an extract to identify both directors and writers by name to the relevant guild. The American Federation of Musicians collects on behalf of its own members. In this case fees may be waived where music appears only as background to a stock shot or where the footage is used for news or obituary purposes. And finally the Screen Actors' Guild demands individual payment to every individual artist and stunt performer in any film. As many artists will have vanished without trace, the production company, through the Guild, must undertake a search for an address and only when a blank has been drawn will the Guild authorise the use of the footage without penalty. If any artist refuses to play or demands an exorbitant fee the footage may not be shown until an arbitration procedure has been followed.

In other words unless a production has access to expert advice and a dedicated copyright department together with long patience and a longer pocket, getting clearance for many feature films is not feasible.

It ought to mentioned here that there are implications for even film societies or college media students. There are complex provisions for the use of copyright in a training or educational context. There is no objection to the use of filmed material for individual study or research, or for the purposes of teaching or criticism. But film and video does still attract copyright if used in any production, even as part of a student project or amateur video. The temptation to play around with footage obtained through a local video shop can be strong. It is a temptation to be resisted.

Not all footage is from the cinema and not all is complicated by US rights. There is a great deal of domestic archive material which has been cleared and is in the hands of a film library. In many old British cinema productions all rights were assigned to the distributors and these archives are now commercially accessible. There are historic collections such as that of the Imperial War Museum, libraries of former television production companies, and a large selection of stock shot libraries some of which advertise collections of copyright-free early movies.

None of them are cheap. Fees depend upon the nature of the production, depending on whether the showing is proposed for national television, regional, closed circuit, interactive, commercial or whatever. At the national television broadcast level the sums are impressive. The cost of any Disney footage (1995) is £2000 a minute for a single showing. Pathé News library charges £8 per second.

The main libraries will have established procedures for charging and the copyright situation may be uncomplicated. But if there is a copyright complication the production company is responsible for picking up the pieces, not the supplier of the footage. For this reason both the ITV companies and the BBC operate by using standard Sequence Licence Agreements (SLAs). A typical SLA takes a form of indemnity to be signed by the supplier of footage and states the following:

- The broadcast company has non-exclusive rights to a specified number of transmissions in return for the agreed licence fee.
- The fee will be based on the duration of the extract finally transmitted, i.e. not footage supplied for consideration or edited during post-production.
- The supplier warrants that it owns the copyright of the film as well as all ancillary rights in both the picture and the sound track.

- The supplier indemnifies the broadcaster against any subsequent claims or damages.
- The material supplied will be supplied in a transmittable format and be of adequate technical quality.

The trouble is that not every supplier will go along with the standard SLA terms. A lot of libraries insist on a minimum royalty regardless of whether or how much of the footage supplied finishes up in the final cut. The National Film Archive has no minimum fee but charges strictly on the duration supplied regardless of transmitted length.

Television companies and advertising agencies will allow access to domestically produced material, but will not undertake to administer any clearances. It will be the job of the licensing company to track down performers.

Different organisations charge in different ways, usually by the second with or without minimum time, sometimes by the 35 mm foot or even the 16 mm foot. To help producers stock shot libraries will normally send VHS copies with time code in vision of likely footage for precise selection. Sometimes these will be charged for, sometimes loaned free if returned by a specific date.

Many libraries store their master material on videotape or even digitally. But a lot of material is on film and this may entail booking an editing bench and a film editor or librarian to supervise the viewing and papering up of films. This can turn film research into an expensive chore. If your final product is likely to be on videotape then copying to the appropriate format will be necessary. If the whole production is to end up on film then duplicate prints and negatives will be required which will entail laboratory fees.

Much footage shot before the 1950s survives on nitrate-based film stock. Nitrate stock is always highly flammable, becomes unstable with age and slowly decays into explosive. Viewing old stock is subject to stringent safety precautions and such viewing may only be done on special premises.

In a similar way videotape, once hailed as the answer to all archiving problems, has turned out to be less reliable than film. Not only do pictures have a tendency to degenerate but the older tapes themselves are subject to decay. On top of this video has existed in a bewildering range of usually incompatible formats. There are currently no fewer than seven in use by British television. Access to a tape might be complicated by the inability to find a machine capable of replaying it.

There are a series of reference works, several now available on CD-ROM covering film and television collections both in the UK and Europe, as well as guides to clearing rights in broadcast and multimedia published by:

The British Universities Film and Video Council
55 Greek Street
London W1V 5LR

The best information source for unearthing the owners of feature film copyright is the British Film Institute. It will help clear copyright on a number of productions although generally it will restrict itself to assistance in checking rights and giving advice.

The BFI also holds a large stills library and can provide prints for a very moderate price. However, most film publicity stills count as integral parts of the production for copyright purposes rather than as ordinary photographs and clearances may not be straightforward. The address is:

The British Film Institute
Film and Video Library
21 Stephen Street
London W1

A good starting point for chasing copyright is to consult *Halliwell's Film Guide*, published by Granada Publishing.

11
MUSIC AND MUSICIANS

The role of music in film and television is so essential that it merits a book to itself. The term 'silent cinema' is profoundly misleading. From the very beginning it was found to be unnerving to watch flickering images with only a clattering projector noise for accompaniment. Long before proper talkies, pictures were viewed with sound, first a soloist at a piano and later with the most sophisticated Wurlitzer organs complete with sound effects. City cinemas sometimes had full pit orchestras.

Contrary to the fond wishes of many television journalists the impact of commentary almost always plays third fiddle to pictures and music plus sound effects in most programmes. Consequently it is a very unusual production that does not use music at some point, if only for opening or closing title sequences.

Apart from music incidental to a location, which raises its own problems and is discussed later, there are three main ways in which a producer or director may acquire music:

- Music may be specially commissioned, composed and recorded to fit the cut pictures.
- It may be taken from commercial gramophone recordings.
- It may be found ready composed or arranged for film and television in a specialist library (production music commonly called mood music).

The use of specially composed music has become far more affordable in recent decades thanks to technological advances and the comparative reduction in the price of equipment. There are now hundreds of small sound studios and companies capable of turning in a very competent job of recording simple music tracks, and no shortage of keen amateur composers complete with sophisticated electronic keyboards and synthesisers. It might seem that composing, arranging and recording a music track can easily be reduced to a one-man operation, but there are drawbacks.

- *Copyright*: if the composer produces unmistakably original work all is fine, but if recognisable melodies or themes from compositions in copyright are used there will be trouble. It is the responsibility of the producer as well as of the composer to make sure that any recognisable song or composition can be cleared. It is important that the composer contractually assigns all synchronisation rights to the production.

- *Union agreements*: there are agreements between the Musicians' Union and the broadcast media. Although synthesisers and electronic music open up enormous possibilities, the union is naturally unhappy at the thought of new technology putting its members out of work. The MU/PACT agreement contains the following clause:

> *Instrumental electronic devices producing the sound of two or more conventional instruments may not be used to displace live recording musicians except where such an instrumental device has an established use by a musical group in connection with its established performance.*

As with the rest of the industry the pace of technological change creates problems for the producer in selecting a recording facility. For corporate or training productions it may be adequate to record directly onto the appropriate format of videotape although the use of DAT (Digital Audio Tape) is becoming standard. There are newer formats enabling recording direct to disk. Decisions about recording, editing and mastering formats will affect both quality and costs. Most of the larger studios belong to the Association of Professional Recording Services (APRS) which will advise on facilities.

 The Association of Professional Recording Services
2 Windsor Square
Silver Street
Reading
Berks RG1 2TH

Most recording studios are listed in:

The Music Week Directory
Spotlight Publications
Ludgate House
245 Blackfriars Road
London SE1 9UR

Knowledge of the relevant Musicians' Union agreements is essential if the producer is not going to run into trouble or be landed with unending financial complications.

Fees are fixed according to the intended use of the track, for example musicians appearing in vision on a nationally transmitted light entertainment show will attract many times the final music bill than out of vision musicians on a regional magazine programme.

There are differing rates for big feature films and low budget British productions. Small groups such as jazz quartets or chamber ensembles are collectively less expensive than an ad hoc assembly of freelance musicians. Contracts may include provision for a single transmission and residual repeat or additional use fees, or may take the form of a one-off combined use fee. Feature productions will normally buy out all rights worldwide when contracting music.

The possible permutations look horrific on paper. But in reality if the producer knows what the possible use of the production is, the amount and nature of the music required, and the budget available there should be no major problem. The first point of reference is:

The Musicians' Union
60/62 Clapham Road
London SW1P 1PH

It is worth pointing out though that not all musicians are represented by the MU. Vocal and instrumental soloists and some chamber ensembles are represented by ISM, the Incorporated Society of Musicians. Other likely members of ISM are orchestral and choral conductors, accompanists and church organists. Most military bands are members of the MU but cathedral choirs probably fall under ISM agreements. Its address is:

The Incorporated Society of Musicians
10 Stratford Place
London W1N 9AE

Music is used to enhance or set the atmosphere of a scene and so the music needs and costs will vary. An evening in a Spanish garden may be appropriately evoked by a solo guitar or a sailing sequence by a harmonica or pipe. Evoking the Charge of the Light Brigade with brass and percussion may work out a lot more costly.

The first priority is for a producer to find a resourceful composer and define how much music is needed for the money available. Composers have no collectively negotiated rates but a Composers' Joint Council in 1993 proposed that incidental music should be charged at between £43 to £135 per minute and title music should be charged at a minimum of £430 regardless of duration. Information about standard contracts may be had from:

The Alliance of Composer Organisations
34 Hanway Street
London W1P 9DE

Composers are represented by a variety of organisations including: the British Academy of Songwriters, Composers and Authors; the Association of Composers; the Composers' Guild of Great Britain; and the Music Copyright Reform Group.

Fortunately for the length of this book they can all be contacted at the Alliance of Composer Organisations address above. There is also a British Music Information Centre at Stratford Place, London. Whilst many feature films have traditionally been accompanied by music from beginning to end most British television productions, including dramas, have been sparing in their use of music often limiting it to opening and closing sequences. The trend though is discernibly towards a greater use of musical soundtracks, probably due to overseas sales and audiences accustomed to US soap operas. At the other end of the television spectrum is the flash magazine programme aimed at a youth audience who are assumed to be unable to concentrate without regular blasts of rock music.

Melodramatic scoring may be essential to a US soap opera. It often serves the purpose of signalling a commercial break. However, directors might keep in mind the musicians' term for compulsively underscoring every mood change – 'Mickey-Mousing'.

If the production has an adequate budget it should be possible to get a full orchestral sound from as few as 14 players with judicious recording and re-mixing. You should not plan for musicians to overdub. If over-dubbing is allowed by MU agreement it will attract an extra fee. Do not ask one trumpet to make subsequent passes over a tape to make four trumpets. However, you may arrange for the trumpet to double on French horn or a clarinettist to play saxophone or oboe so long as each is on a single pass of a tape.

The length of studio sessions for musicians is defined by union agreement. Without taking into account the many provisos it can be assumed that a standard session will be three hours long with a 15 minute rest break included. Experienced music producers reckon that the maximum final recorded track that can be achieved effectively in one session is between 20 and 25 minutes.

Because of the specialist knowledge involved in commissioning music and clearing rights the British Film Commission recommends that productions with heavy music requirements employ a specialist executive music producer. Apart from getting the best deal for the budget and avoiding copyright disasters a music producer will explore the secondary sale of recorded soundtracks with record companies and possibly offset some of the initial music costs. A music producer can also handle the delicate business of reconciling the composer's requirements with the needs of the recording engineers and the requirements of musicians. Music producers may be located through the usual reference directories; otherwise contact:

 The Society of Producers of Applied Music
Birchwood House
Storridge
Malvern
Worcestershire WR13 5EZ

Commercial recorded music

Enforcing the copyright on a book is a comparatively straightforward matter. The evidence for any plagiarism is there in permanent form. With music the problems are infinitely more complex. The pirating of a musical score or the words of a lyric is fairly easily traced, but a performance is an ephemeral event. Recorded music as part of a sound track may be fragmentary or mixed with other sound effects and dialogue. There may exist a number of near identical recordings of the same music. The latest development of sampling, where a sound studio may strip off and reuse tracks from earlier recordings further complicates the matter. And most music making is in itself a complicated cooperative enterprise. There may be different copyrights in the composition, the arrangement, the lyrics and the performance as well as copyright in the recording itself. All of which adds up to the practical advice that if a director is set upon incorporating any commercially available music in the sound track plenty of time needs to be allocated to establish clearances. A single dissident member of a recording group can pull the rug from under a production at the last moment. In film editing terms this can have awful consequences. Whereas commissioned music is composed to fit the pictures, pictures are best fine cut to fit the tracks of pre-recorded music. A last minute substitution of an alternative piece of music can have artistically unpleasant consequences, and the replacement of one version by another at a different tempo can use up a lot of time in extra post-production making music and picture fit.

There are four main copyright protection organisations, as discussed below.

The British Phonographic Industry (BPI)

The BPI is the main trade association of the recording industry with over 170 corporate members. Although the BPI represents the major record labels it does not generally administer rights clearances, and of late much of its energies have been devoted to fighting commercial piracy and bootleg recordings. It is, however, of importance to broadcasting companies as it is party to blanket agreements with the main networks. Independent productions should be covered by such agreements but there are labels not represented by BPI and using these can create problems

Licences to use a commercial recording must *always* be obtained directly from the record company concerned. Although a number of labels are grouped together as parts of major companies like Polygram, Sony and Warner, many labels remain autonomous, and there may be amalgamations and take-overs in progress. Approaching the holding company is not always the quickest route.

Contact:

 British Phonographic Industry
25 Savile Row
London W1X 1AA

Phonographic Performance Limited (PPL) and Video Performance Limited (VPL)

PPL protects the rights of the recording companies over the public playing, cable diffusion and broadcasting of their music. Anyone who wishes to play commercial recordings whether Classic FM or a publican with a juke box needs to be licensed with PPL. Fees are normally negotiated with the broadcasters or players of music according to usage rather than producers. As broadcasters are covered by blanket agreements PPL is not likely to make great problems for production companies. The blanket agreements are administered by PPL on behalf of BPI. Although around 95 per cent of British labels are represented by PPL / BPI there are some which are not, as indeed are many foreign labels. It remains the responsibility of the individual producer to confirm clearances.

PPL has a sister organisation Video Performance Limited (VPL). Its main concern is the distribution of music videos, particularly pop videos, in public places such as pubs and night clubs as well as cable, satellite and terrestrial broadcasts. VPL has assigned rights from its member companies to license the inclusion of pop videos in other films or television productions. PPL spends a considerable amount of effort in litigation enforcing its rights and revenue comes to several millions annually. Two thirds goes back to the record companies but the remainder plugs a hole in the complex musical copyright arrangements. Musicians themselves lack comprehensive protection. There is no effective way in which the army of individual recording musicians can be protected so PPL operates an ex *gratia* fund on their behalf paid either to credited groups and performers via the member companies of PPL, or through a general lump sum for the welfare of the rest paid to the MU.

Although PPL and VPL have traditionally been aggressively protective of their members' rights, it has become clear that the awesome problems of copyright clearance have deterred TV comp-anies from using their members' work at all. The problem has become particularly acute with pop music promotional videos. To make these more accessible in 1996 VPL has launched a subsidiary, 'The Music Mall', which has a database of tens of thousands of videos and will advise producers on availability. It will arrange both clearances and offers a discounted tape duplication service.

Both PPL and VPL are based at:

Ganton House
14–22 Ganton Street
London W1V 1LB

The Performing Right Society (PRS)

Throughout the nineteenth century it was generally held that once a piece of music had been published anybody could sing, play copy or record it to their heart's content. According to legend a bunch of aggrieved composers replied by touring cafes and restaurants with resident orchestras and refusing to pay for their drinks until the management paid for their music. Dramatic gestures were one thing but they hardly laid down a basis for the regular recompense of composers or publishers.

After much lobbying in the UK the 1911 Copyright Act gave composers the exclusive right to the public performance of their works. The Act did not say how composers were to collect their money. That problem was solved in 1914 by the creation of the PRS as a collections society.

Today the PRS represents songwriters, lyricists, arrangers, music publishers and even poets whose work may have been set to music. Music users, whether broadcasters, concerts halls or the local hairdresser would find it impossible to negotiate performing rights for every piece of music they use and the system works to the advantage of all.

The way the system works is as follows:

- The composer or publisher assigns the rights to the PRS.
- The PRS is in a position to take legal action to prevent unlicensed music being used and so polices the music users.
- Music users pay an annual fee, in most cases a blanket fee which entitles them to play any PRS music.
- The PRS shares out, as equitably as possible, the resulting revenues.

Almost all music is cleared through PRS, but not absolutely all. If there are doubts it will pay to check. PRS inspectors are extremely active and there are regional as well as national offices.

There are over 40 different tariffs covering every music user from BBC national transmissions to the musical holding systems on office telephone systems and the music accompanying TV engineering test cards.

Producers working for broadcasting companies probably need worry no more. The company will have a negotiated PRS blanket licence. The only way this impinges on the production will be the requirement to submit a detailed dope sheet for every piece of music used in a production. This, however, is also a requirement of the MCPS (Mechanical Copyright Protection Society – see below).

Broadcasters pay fees according to their estimated audience reach. National terrestrial transmissions are calculated at 100 per cent of the agreed hourly fee and smaller organisations are discounted accordingly. For instance in 1991 Thames Television paid at a 19.4 per cent ratio, local commercial radio stations between 5 per cent and 9 per cent and BBC Radio Orkney a mere 0.04 per cent.

It is probably only in the corporate or training sector of the market that clients may need to be aware of PRS requirements. A standard corporate contract will state that the production company hands over the master tape free of all copyright problems. Altercations will follow if the client then gives public performances of a work at unlicensed venues or has failed to make returns about the use of the music or discovers that music can not be cleared by PRS.

Currently the PRS collects over £50 million a year in licences for public performances and around £170 million in other royalties of which a major part come from radio and television. It either administers or is affiliated to sister organisations worldwide.

Composers and publishers assign to the PRS the three following performing rights:

- The right to perform a work.
- The right to broadcast a work.
- The right to transmit it via cable.

The PRS does not license the right to record or dub music, except for specially composed scores. Dubbing is the mechanical right and is administered by the MCPS. The PRS also retains rights on behalf of its members and licenses theatrical releases in the USA. As a rule the PRS does not license 'Grand Right' performances which include dramatico-musical works such as stage musicals, opera or ballet.

The Mechanical Copyright Protection Society (MCPS)

The PRS only grants permission for the performance or broadcast of a work. It does not license others to make a recording of a work or copy or dub it from an existing recording, or in the words of the Copyright Act 'to reproduce it in any material form'. This covers both original recordings and the use of previously recorded music in film or broadcasting. These rights are known as the

Mechanical Rights.
The forerunner of the MCPS was set up before the 1911 Copyright Act. The name reflects the state of technology of the time. The familiar way to record a work was on punched paper rolls on mechanical pianos or punch cards on street barrel organs. But the wax cylinder was already established and copyright holders had an eye on the emerging record industry.

For a long period revenues were collected by means of a duty stamp attached to the cardboard covers of shellac disks. Latterly the MCPS logo has been incorporated in the design of disks and the jackets of cassettes and CDs.

At present the MCPS levies a duty of 8.5 per cent of the published retail price for records and tapes. The revenue from recordings for home listening remain the major source of income but the ever expanding broadcast area gives increasing prominence to non-retail revenue.

Clearing mechanical rights can give today's producers real headaches. There was a time when all television was produced either by the BBC or ITV and the programme makers were nearly all employees of one or other of the broadcast companies. Rights were either dealt with by blanket agreements or negotiated by dedicated departments.

Times have changed. Whether operating in broadcast or non-broadcast areas the producer is likely to find that all responsibility for clearing mechanical rights, and incorporating the costs in the programme budget, is his or hers alone. So whatever the nature of the production concerned, if there is any possibility of using commercial music in a sound track it is vital that the MCPS Non-Retail Licensing Department is contacted at an early stage.

Clearances have to be obtained in advance of transmission and royalties paid up front with licences only issued within 28 days of payment being received.

The MCPS Negotiator will undertake to try to identify the copyright holder, obtain approval for usage and negotiate an appropriate fee. This may not be possible in all cases. Some recording companies, for example EMI, have reserved the right to negotiate their own permissions and fees. And there is a final copyright, in the disk or tape itself, which will entail the producer getting direct permission from the record company.

The MCPS can only act as an honest broker and collector of royalties. It cannot promise that clearances will be forthcoming. UK only rights will be easier to clear than world rights. Broadcast companies have long since come to regard world rights for most major US record labels as being in effect impossible to clear.

There is no fixed scale of fees for using commercial recordings. The copyright holders will set their price according to the type of programme, the nature of the chosen music and the proposed means of exploitation. Before approaching the negotiator, then, the director is asked to provide MCPS with the following details:

- Production title.
- Composer/author/arranger.
- Artists.
- Publisher.
- Proposed duration.
- Context of use.
- Production company.
- Production client.
- Production title.
- Production format.
- Programme subject matter.
- Territories of distribution.
- Anticipated sales of copies if appropriate.

Quoted prices will be per 30 second unit and valid for three months. Any change in the proposed exploitation of the production will need a re-negotiated fee.

Production music

Help is at hand.

Production music, commonly called 'mood music' or 'library music', comprises specially composed and recorded music tracks tailored for film, video or audio visual presentations and guaranteed clear of copyright complications by MCPS.

A rate card is available and a licence will be automatically granted in the usual time scale on receipt of the programme details outlined above. Before applying for a licence to use production music the MCPS will expect the production company or individual director to sign a code of conduct committing the signatory to abide by the procedures laid down by the MCPS. Music licence forms and music log sheets are then issued.

There are 60 recorded music libraries affiliated to MCPS. There are tens of thousands of music and effects tracks available ranging from drum taps at different tempi and electronic sounds to full orchestral recordings of classical symphonies.

There is an enormous variety of original ethnic recordings and specially composed short stings for programme junctions and commercial breaks.

Despite the range available it is surprising how frequently the same pieces are heard and this does highlight a small problem. Production music is available to everyone. Quite a number of famous television and radio signature tunes originated on a library disk. Anyone may use the same tune for another programme or for satirical purpose unless a special exclusivity agreement can be negotiated with the library.

At one time library music was distinguished by the most awful drivel but today there are superb recordings by distinguished composers and performers who often put their names to their tracks. In other cases well reputed performers or groups appear under whimsical pseudonyms. A few hours or even days researching library music can be an encouraging activity for directors depressed by the obstacles to getting clearance for their favourite commercial recordings.

It is no fault of the record libraries if directors ruin their productions through an addiction to musical garbage. The mark of the majority of corporate videos is a ceaseless bombardment of inappropriate library music from beginning to end. Presumably it is put there in the hope of spicing up the turgid content or to conceal the inadequacies of location sound and the audio mix. There are directors and producers with tin ears. As music so often conditions the cutting of the pictures, the job of music selection is better left to a competent picture editor.

Libraries may sometimes sell a complete collection or a selection of their work on CD or will allow their disks out on loan for a selection to be made. In the case of bona fide users like broadcasting companies, facility houses and even film schools, the loan is sometimes in reality a gift. The libraries only get their revenue when a music track is used so it pays to distribute the disks widely. Music libraries will of course offer advice and suggestions in the selection of suitable tracks but it will be as well for any production unit to collect the printed catalogues of a number of companies first. Libraries will naturally only recommend their own recordings.

Of late there have become available numbers of 'sound-alike' disks some available through record libraries and some commercially distributed through chain stores and supermarkets. In essence they are copy recordings of musical numbers or classical exerpts performed by generally anonymous ensembles. In most cases copyright has already been cleared with the original composers and performers or the material will be itself out of copyright. Sound-alikes from MCPS libraries are cleared in the usual way. Those on the retail market need to be treated with a certain caution particularly if they happen to turn up in street markets. Piracy, re-packaging and unlicensed sampling are international rackets.

So widespread are library recordings and so trouble free that many programme makers in the past have treated them not just as bargains but as though they were free. The budgetary systems of broadcast companies sometimes encouraged this impression. The MCPS rate card shows otherwise.

In 1996 up to 30 seconds in a commercial with world rights costs £1515 per use on terrestrial channels and £1020 on satellite, though at the bottom of a rapidly sliding scale a corporate video could buy European rights for as little as £18 per 30 seconds. All enquiries should be addressed to:

 The Mechanical Copyright Protection Society
Elgar House
41 Streatham High Road
London SW16 1ER

Incidental music

Documentary makers wisely often choose to keep to music actually recorded by themselves on location. This is frequently far more effective than the artifice of using commercial disks or library music to heighten a scene. And the production ought to be free of copyright payments.

The nature of the incidental music needs to be considered before use because it must be shown to be incidental. A brass band playing during a rehearsal of the Trooping of the Colour is incidental in a documentary context. But were the director to ask the band to repeat an item, or play a particular number, or in any way perform to the camera, the performance would turn into a concert and the whole payment can of worms spilled, starting with an MU fee for each bandsman.

A street busker may happily agree to play for a small gratuity but if the music he plays is a pop tune in copyright and it is clear that it is a deliberate performance for television and not some unavoidable background atmosphere then the production could be infringing copy-right. It is unlikely that the Beatles would invoke copyright against a busker playing 'Yellow Submarine' or the busker demand full MU rates for his appearance. It is just as unlikely that either would seek an injunction against a genuine documentary. But sequences shot at concerts or night clubs or even street festivals can be completely different. Artists' managers may forbid any filming of a public performance, even some verses of a song at a charity event, if they have not been consulted or contracted in the first place.

Traditional music, either gathered during a shoot or taken from other local recordings, need not be trouble-free either. Much folk music may be centuries out of copyright, but a particular arrangement may not. Composers of every type have incorporated folk airs in their music, and a lot of currently recognisable folk tunes are in fact re-worked modern versions. Currently copyright lasts for 50 years from the end of the calendar year in which the recording was first released, possibly soon to be extended to 70 years. So something which just sounds ancient and so with luck goes down on the music log as 'trad. no fee' might still be someone's property. Likewise a field of Andean nose flute music might seem to be freely available, or more cynically there will be no way of paying either the artists or composer, but the musical anthropologist concerned can claim, copyright in the original recording.

Copyright can throw up some surprises. 'Happy Birthday' is sung on the right occasions worldwide, even in Beirut, Beijing and Guandong. Worldwide acceptance does not bestow antiquity. The tune is still in copyright and is published by EMI.

A traditional tune may be non-copyright but the lyrics may be covered. Similarly poetry may be set to music and either one or the other may remain in copyright.

There is now the possibility of re-working and digitally re-mastering old recordings. The fact that a music hall number was recorded on a cylinder a century ago does not mean a re-recorded digital version is copyright free. In programmes of review or criticism a defence against copyright is the concept of 'fair dealing'. Fair dealing is a slippery legal concept which crops up in a number of contexts. In outline it allows a programme to use reasonable illustrative extracts of work to either review a current production or retrospectively look at a career or historical period. What duration of extract in which context counts as fair dealing is hard to define, certainly the use of whole acts or potted versions of works would infringe copyright.

Grand right

And finally there are 'grand right' productions. These are recordings of musical performances which are part of theatrical productions including stage musicals, operas and ballets. Dramatico-musical works are specifically excluded from any of the blanket agreements made with the copyright protection organisations. Recordings of such performances raise fearsome problems through the mixed copyright status of singers, actors, orchestras , dancers, arrangers, etc. A few of the points to watch are:

- A libretto has a separate copyright from the music.
- A libretto which is a translation of an original will have an additional copyright in the later version.
- A re-arranged classical score may have copyright protection in the new orchestration or a novel arrangement.
- The choreography of a ballet or stage musical is copyrighted, and so are the sub-titles used during foreign language productions.

As a postscript none of these considerations is half so insurmountable as the problems inherent in trying to clear rights for the use film clips of numbers from US film musicals based on stage originals. This is specialist area. The general advice is don't even think about it.

12

ART AND DESIGN

Paintings, drawings and designs are subject to copyright. Frequently so are things as diverse as brochures, record and book covers, labels and even pub signs. New fonts and typefaces are subject to copyright and much ingenuity goes into designing and buying rights for fonts to go into computer programs along with the few familiar fonts in the public domain. Three-dimensional objects can be protected by copyright including original costume design (think of the distinctive costumes of children's science fiction series and the subsequent marketing of toys, games and fancy dress outfits). Sculptures, stage sets and architectural models and plans are protected. The Coca Cola Corporation established a precedent when it obtained copyright on the shape of a bottle.

All cartoon characters are copyright and since the income from licensing the use of such characters often far exceeds the income derived from the original cartoons this copyright is vigorously enforced. The merest glimpse of an unlicensed Donald Duck or Bugs Bunny will bring down the legal wrath of the Disney Corporation or Time Warner, the two biggest players in film and television in the world.

Copyright exists even if original work is part of a greater entity. For example an animated title sequence will attract its own copyright unless rights have been assigned by the designer to the producer of the entire programme.

Prints and engravings remain in copyright for 50 years, perhaps henceforth 70 years, from the death of the author although a past complication has been the discovery of 'lost' works in which case a new copyright was created from the date of first publication.

If copyright were to be enforced to the least detail life would become quite impossible for the programme maker. It would be necessary to obtain clearance before showing every painted shop front or illustrated tee-shirt. Every window display, advertising poster or magazine cover would be a potential trap. As elsewhere the concept of 'fair dealing' comes to the rescue. It will usually be held to be dealing fairly if the copyright work is on permanent public display, so there is no problem of performers turning up by a statue in the park. This would probably not apply however if the statue in question became the subject of the programme itself. Because a work by a contemporary artist is on permanent exhibition in the Tate Gallery, it does not give you the right to use it as part of your title sequence though you might get away with fair dealing if the picture passed in view during an item about the gallery itself. This example does illustrate the point that the owner of an original work is often not the copyright holder. Reproduction rights may or may not have been assigned at the time of sale in the case of living artists. Museums and galleries do not usually acquire copyright with the acquisition of ownership.

Much depends on whether the appearance of the material is truly incidental to the action or deliberately included as part of an overall design. Of course a great deal of graphic design is itself intended for publicity purposes and the copyright owners will be only too delighted to grant permission for its use, at least after their public relations officers have been assured about the context. A far greater cause for concern of late has been the growth of 'product placement' whereby directors and designers wilfully include products, advertisements and art work into TV programmes in return for money.

Using material, with the exception of original photographs, for critical and review purposes is legitimate. The amount of illustrative copyright material that may be used is disputable.

Authors and publishers have an interest in keeping such a proportion as low as is commensurate with the publicity value, producers may have an interest in exploiting material to the longest permissible duration. Certainly if illustrative material is used it should have been obtained fairly, full acknowledgement of the artist should be made at the time and the use of the material should not impinge in any way on the sales or profits of the artist. Journalists and topical programme directors have an additional defence of 'public interest'. A contentious art exhibition, an enquiry into advertising, a scandal involving an artist, questions of pornography, disputed attribution or obituaries are subjects where a the programme maker may claim public interest against copyright infringement.

Note: photographs derived from a still frame of a film or TV programme are protected as films, not under copyright rules for photographs, and the 'fair dealing' excuse might not apply.

Artists, photographers and designers have their own copyright collection and protection society:

 The Design and Artists Copyright Society
Parchment House
13 Northburgh Street
London EC1V 0AH

Photographs

Still photographs are the form of graphics most frequently required by programme makers. Photographs are reproducable by their very nature and establishing the owner may be difficult particularly if the original negatives have been lost. Many published photographs may have been given no printed attribution in their original published form.

The first Copyright Act of 1911 dated copyright as 50 years from the date on which a photograph was taken. Even at that date the attribution of many photographs could not be established nor could the precise date of the exposure. Fortunately time has taken care of most early copyrights.

Under the revised Act of 1957 the rules were changed and henceforth copyright was to be dated from the date of the first publication or broadcast.

This created problems for picture researchers. A photograph from a family album or private collection might be a century old but unpublished. A new copyright could therefore be established. Who held that copyright was of course another matter. In the absence of a clear bequest which members of a family might hold the rights to a family photo album?

The 1957 Act tried to simplify matters a little by granting copyright to whoever paid for the original film in the camera. This put photographers in a disadvantaged position compared to writers or painters. Photographers on the payroll of any employer, even as freelances, had no hold on the copyright in their work.

The Copyright Act of 1988 has brought photographers into line with other authors. Copyright is vested in the person who 'creates the work' i.e. the photographer. Copyright extends for 50 years from the death of the photographer. It has been jokingly suggested that if you hand your camera to a third party to take a holiday snap the copyright belongs to the stranger and remains until 50, or possibly now 70 years after the stranger has gone to meet his maker.

The new law improved the copyright situation for non-professional and freelance photographers. Most photographs, however, are commissioned by newspapers, periodicals or publicity agencies and if the photographer is contractually paid for specific commissions the copyright will belong to the commissioner. A photographer for a newspaper cannot sell his work to a rival whether or not the images were published by his employer. A freelance shooting speculatively might do so.

On the other hand either photographer might retain some rights in the future use of the original material. A photographer might retain copyright in the use of a photograph for a different purpose to that for which it was first commissioned. A photographer might benefit from the exploitation of an image shot for publication in a journal but subsequently exploited for poster advertising or television purposes. Moral rights may apply except in the case of staff employees. Increasingly photographers in print media insist on a personal credit alongside their images.

So selecting a picture for use in a television programme might still land a producer with problems if it is not clear whether or to whom the rights have been assigned. A good example of the potential problems is found in the question of using wedding photographs. Even if the pictures are those of a professional wedding photographer specifically commissioned by the happy couple then the copyright on the photograph belongs to the photographer and not the married couple. If the photographs are derived from a local newspaper photographer then copyright will depend on the status of the photographer. Was he on the staff or was he a stringer shooting on spec., with a view to selling his work to both a newspaper and the wedding party? Was the picture the work of a friend or relative and effectively a gift to the couple though the copyright would remain the property of the photographer and not the owner of the prints? Remember that wedding photoraphs are often liberally distributed amongst relatives.

An illustration of the problems is the case of *Daily Mail* versus *Daily Express* 1987. The *Daily Mail* bought exclusive rights to a set of wedding photographs from a husband whose pregnant wife was being kept alive on a life support machine. The *Express* obtained copies of the same photographs and maintained that the *Mail* could not have exclusive rights as copyright was held jointly by husband and wife and exclusive copyright could be assigned only by both acting together. The court upheld the principle that copyright was jointly held by husband and wife. In this very particular case the case of the *Mail* was upheld on the very sensible grounds that the wife was clinically dead and in no position to contest title to the pictures. The subsequent 1988 Act recognising the copyright of the actual photographer would further muddy the waters in any re-run of such a case.

But even in less macabre circumstances there may be reasons for hesitating before publishing personal photographs apart from copyright. The subjects of photographs may find pictures of early indiscretions and events embarrassing or insulting at a later date or in another context. A confidentiality is presumed to have existed between a sitter and a photographer and publication may be held to be defamatory.

Photographers are represented and advised on copyright matters by:

The British Photographers' Liaison Committee
Domingo Street
London EC1 0TA

The best selections of photographic and other pictorial material are found in the 200 or more picture libraries in Great Britain. They range in scale from enormous newspaper archives to small specialist collections of subjects as diverse as space exploration, botany and theatrical prints. Apart from supplying their own copyright material they often act as agencies for freelance photographers contributing to specialist fields. In the latter case the programme maker must be sure that rights can be properly cleared through the library. In most cases the picture library will have a rate card and a guarantee that all pictures supplied will be free of other copyright problems.

This may not apply to collections and libraries run by public bodies and local government authorities. Many of these include privately loaned or donated collections and many of the prints included may be copies of well-known originals. So copyright problems are still possible. For example, the National Film Archive has an excellent library of cinema stills and publicity photographs but cannot undertake copyright clearance for publication. Different collections charge in different ways and picture research can turn out to be expensive as well as time consuming if it is not well planned. Fees come in several forms:

- *Access fees*: a sort of temporary reading room ticket charged if you wish to do your own research in a collection or archive normally not accessible to the public.
- *Search fees*: payable to the owners or archivists of a collection for conducting a search for specific stills. Charges will vary according to the time and effort involved which itself will depend on the obscurity of the subject matter and the appropriateness of the brief. Asking for pictures of the jungle is rather different to asking for a shot including a particular tree. Charges for extensive searches may be high so it may pay to ask for an estimate first.
- *Service fees*: cover the costs of handling, packing and despatch. A charge of up to £50 would not be unusual. Normal postage is obviously the cheapest option when there is no urgency but a courier service might be assumed necessary by a librarian.
- *Rental fees*: are payable for the days during which you retain

the pictures. Many libraries make a nominal charge or lend material free for a limited period and thereafter a series of fines are imposed just like those for an unreturned library book. Extensions can often be granted but going over a return date can be very expensive indeed. Fines are fixed at a punitive level and after a short period you will be deemed to have lost or stolen the picture and be charged a full replacement cost. A charge of several hundred pounds for replacing quite unremarkable material is perfectly possible.

- *Reproduction fees*: are a charge for reproducing materials from a collection in a programme or publication. For example many art galleries will retain high quality transparencies of paintings in their collections where copyright in the originals no longer exists. Photography is usually banned by museums and galleries.

- *Reference fees*: apply to the supply of materials to design directors, graphic artists, wardrobe designers and such who need material for reference without any intention of publication. Distinct scales of fees may exist.

There are both ethical and practical problems which can arise from using old material which has previously been published in another form. Many libraries include picture collections from nineteenth-century illustrated magazines, early advertisements or political cartoons. As similar material will exist in different places the temptation to cheat over attribution and avoid payment is present. The deviousness is not worth the effort. The offended library will refuse to do business with you again and word gets around. Most archives and collections are affiliated to:

 The British Association of Picture Libraries and Agencies (BAPLA)
13 Woodberry Crescent
London N10 1PJ

It is possible that a photograph or print is to be found in a book but with no attribution to a photographer or artist. The director must protect against copyright problems by making a proper search starting with publisher's records and, when all else fails, attributing the last known source. If a copyright holder does emerge the payment of a suitable fee should settle the matter without legal action.

The Copyright Act extends the same protection to still photographs as it does to films and you may not take a picture of a picture with impunity any more than you may take images from a videotape or television screen.

Crown copyright

All sorts of Government-derived material comes under a quite distinct body of copyright. Coins, Ordnance Survey maps and bank notes are all Crown copyright as are all guides and publications issued by Her Majesty's Stationery Office. In the case of bank notes convincing copy currency is illegal and if close-up shots of notes are needed the money has to be real. The security problems involved on set have prematurely aged more than one television director.

The Royal Family has effectively got copyright in itself. Even widely distributed photographs of a Coronation service may not be used without Palace permission, which is by no means automatically given.

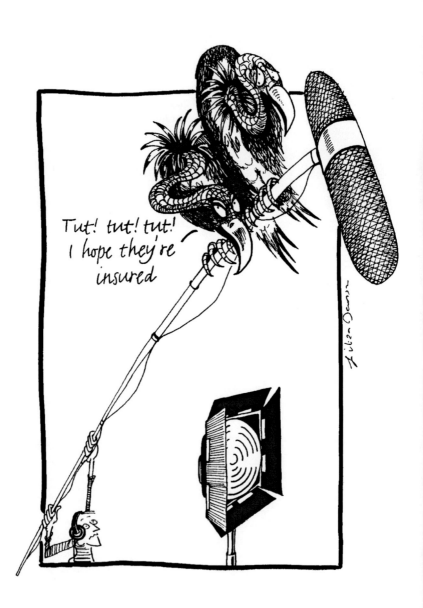

13

SAFETY MATTERS

Working in television can be dangerous. News cameramen and war correspondents pursue hazardous careers by definition, but even mundane little productions can run into unexpected trouble. The reasons are not hard to find. No two locations and no two productions are ever the same and so there is no foolproof safety procedure which fits all circumstances.

Television is teamwork, but teams change during the process and are often made up of individuals who do not regularly work together. Television productions are always under budget and dead-line pressures, and the temptation to cut corners and take chances is often irresistible. Lights, cables and camera mounts as well as a host of other items from ladders to hair lacquer can be lethal.

The law makes no exceptions for television. All employers and employees are covered by the Health and Safety at Work Act 1974. This has been amplified since 1993 by the Management of Health and Safety at Work Regulations which harmonise UK law with various EU directives. The main provisions of the regulations are:

- Employers have to carry out an assessment of the risks arising out of their working environment and review these whenever the nature of the work changes.
- Risk assessment should be followed by appropriate protective measures.
- Management must be able to show their compliance with the regulations. In any enterprise employing five or more people arrangements must be recorded. There should also be one or more health and safety officers designated.
- Employees must be given full information on any risks, safety measures and emergency procedures. This includes temporary freelance staff and contractors. Permanent staff should receive formal health and safety training.
- Employers must establish procedures for dealing with imminent dangerous situations. This may be as familiar as an office fire drill, but during location filming it extends to procedures during any stunt or hazardous special effect.

There is a clear difference between the situation of working on location and working in the well regulated conditions of a studio or film stage. In the latter case working conditions approximate to those on a factory floor and there will normally be fire officers, and possibly even full time safety officers in attendance.

Studios are so conscious of safety regulations that heated arguments over fire lane obstruction or degrees of fire proofing for sets are not unknown. The ungracious description of fire and safety officers as 'programme prevention officers' has been heard in one large broadcasting organisation.

Studios are usually the property of broadcast companies or facility houses which will have their own safety procedures and conditions. There are occasions when a studio is rented as 'dry hire' i.e. the four walls and equipment are rented but the operating personnel are provided by the producers. In such cases the studio owners are counted as landlords and it is their responsibility to brief the production company about all health and safety measures and also to monitor the actvities of their tenants.

Responsibility for studio safety is normally split. The senior engineer will be responsible for all technical safety. Responsibility for the safety of performers and those working on the studio floor will be delegated to a production manager, assistant director or floor manager. If either of these regards an activity as potentially hazardous they have the right to overrule the director and suspend operations until proper measures have been taken. This is of course a very delicate position. On many productions the director has far less experience than the rest of his or her colleagues, as well as feeling under the greatest pressure and having the most at stake. But on several occasions, serious accidents or fatalities have happened when directors have demanded, and unwisely been given, their own way over safety.

Warning
The most important thing to remember is that health and safety legislation is criminal law. Injury will certainly involve insurance investigations and probably civil action for damages against a production company. But the Health and Safety Executive will bring criminal prosecutions against individuals as well as organisations where the legal requirements have been neglected. Penalties can be severe and involve imprisonment as well as unlimited fines.

Employees are still responsible for taking reasonable care of their own safety and that of those they work with. This includes giving full cooperation to those directly responsible for health and safety in a unit, not interfering with safety equipment or ignoring instructions for its use, reporting any dangerous situation promptly, maintaining acceptable standards of hygiene particularly where hazardous substances are used and, to quote PACT, 'There is a duty to act responsibly and refrain from horseplay at work. Others can be put at risk by irresponsible behaviour.'

Responsibility for health and safety with small documentary or current affairs crews is usually assumed to be that of the director or the journalist in charge. Cameramen can and do refuse to do anything they consider to be dangerously daft. As many stories depend upon unpredictable circumstances, common sense may have to take priority over formal hazard assessment. But macho displays on the small screen can attract the attention of the Health and Safety Inspectorate. A reporter shown on a high place without an obvious safety harness or a presenter not wearing appropriate eye protection or protective clothing in an industrial setting can prompt complaints and a request for an inquiry.

The law does take account of the custom and practice of the industry. A reporter in a war zone can be expected to face hazards greater than those faced by the production secretary. But both are subject to health and safety regulations appropriate to the industry. Throughout the civil wars in what was Yugoslavia, probably the most dangerous area for reporters ever, the broadcasting companies constantly reiterated the absolute priority of personal safety. An ordinary secretary in the meantime has problems. From the end of 1996 all computer work stations will be subject to stringent regulations concerning health provisions for habitual users of VDUs including lighting, leg room and seating. Work will have to be planned to take account of breaks away from VDU work. Employers will be obliged to provide eye tests on request and to pay for the cost of spectacles as well as for regular subsequent tests. The definition of 'habitual user' is imprecise but as almost everyone employed in television production spends considerable time at a computer, there must be widespread implications for employers. The regulations also apply to self-employed workers.

Health and Safety regulations fill volumes. On location you are under an obligation to be conversant with other peoples' regulations as well as those of your own employer. It is up to each employer to draw up a detailed schedule and it is possible that regulations in similar locations may vary or even apear contradictory. One hospital may implement its regulations in quite a different way from another and when filming in other peoples' environments it pays to keep checking what may be permitted. The specific high risk areas of shooting in the air or on roads and boats are dealt with elsewhere, but almost any working situation involves some hazard.

Television companies may insist upon the completion of hazard assessment forms by a member of a production team before authorising a shoot. This implies in most cases a recce, even a brief one, on the day and a written report on potential hazards.

Such paperwork demonstrates awareness of the law by employees and effective compliance by the employer. Cynics might observe that once a hazard assessment form is not completed, and safety measures still prove inadequate, the responsibility for any accident is down to the individual and the company can wash its hands.

Hazard assessment has to take account of:

● the probability of an accident;
● the possible consequences;
● any means of reducing or removing the risk;
● any possible protective measures;
● availability of specific procedures or expert assistance to cope with the hazard.

It is accepted that there may have to be a trade-off between cost and risk. It costs little to hire hard hats for everyone on a building site or life jackets for a sea-going craft considering the severity of the risk in the event of an accident. Ordering ear defenders for a short item on church bells might be over cautious. If safety precautions must be taken it is the responsibility of the producer to budget for the neccessary time and money.

In short, whether the project is a battle scene or a cooking programme there is no defence in saying 'nobody told me' or 'I thought everyone knew'. Whether the risk is impalement on a pike or a burn from a hot plate the risks have to be assesssed and every bruise or burn subsequently formally recorded and reported.

The areas of responsibility are awesome in scope and almost any company will have detailed provisions to cover specific areas like electrical safety, fire precautions, lifting heavy objects, ventilation and lighting.

Ten areas of concern for those working on a television production are suggested for reference. The list is far from comprehensive.

● You are responsible for the safety and maintenance of all equipment.
● You are responsible for the handling and storage of all

materials used. This obviously includes pyrotechnics and firearms but also many quite familiar substances. Stage cosmetics may contain flammable solvents and aerosols may be a health hazard in unventilated places.

- You are responsible for ensuring safe access, emergency exit routes and fire lanes. External entrances or exits should never be blocked by vehicles. Fire doors should not be jammed open and left unattended. Cables, wherever possible, should not cross corridors or staircases or should be thoroughly taped down and either supervised or clearly signed by hazard warnings.

- You are responsible for the general welfare of your crew. This means ensuring that proper washing facilities and lavatories are available, providing first aid equipment, and ensuring that heating, lighting and ventilation in workplaces is satisfactory.

- You are responsible for the safety inspection of equipment. Studio hoists, camera cranes and mountings must be regularly inspected for their payloads and the safety of hydraulics. Certificates must be issued. Private and commercial vehicles are subject to Ministry of Transport inspection and certification. You may be responsible at second hand for the sea worthiness of boats or air worthiness of aircraft. The proper fire proofing of sets, props wigs and costumes is your responsibility.

- You are responsible for the professional competence of personnel. The risks arising from using non-trained stunt artists or asking performers to do things beyond their professional qualifications has been mentioned. It is your responsibility to ask for documentary evidence of competence and this applies to drivers, skippers and pilots as well as presenters and actors. 'He said he could do it' or 'it was his own idea' are not good defences against charges of negligence.

- You are responsible for proper planning and proper communications. Accidents are most likely when rehearsals are skimped or carried out without the full attention of the whole unit and when there is a sudden change of plan which is not clearly communicated all round.

- You are responsible for taking specific precautions when shooting at night particularly near roads, railways and docks; for maintaining liaison with rescue and emergency services, and for ensuring that lights do not dazzle.

- You are responsible for the provision of all safety equipment and protective clothing as well as safety spectacles, ear defenders, seat-belts or special footwear.

- You are responsible for the prior inspection of all stairs, ladders, scaffolding or rostra which may have to take the payload of a crew or performers. This applies as much to a rickety staircase in a bell tower as to custom-built studio audience seating. Assessing the safety of locations is often a job for a specialist saftey officer, particularly when old or derelict buildings are being considered.

There are branches of the Health and Safety Executive in most regions. For general enquiries the headquarters are:

 The Health and Safety Executive
Chepstow Place
Westbourne Grove
London W2 4TF

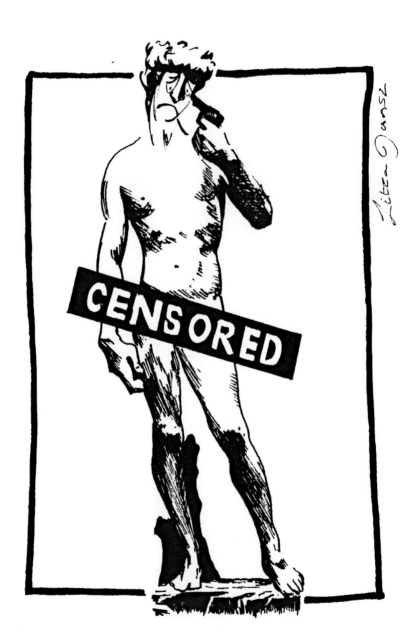

14
MORE TROUBLE WITH THE LAW

Defamation

The consequence of defaming someone is the nightmare of the print journalist and increasingly that of the television producer. The reason is first that recourse to actions for defamation seem to be increasingly fashionable and secondly that the financial consequences can be utterly ruinous.

So slippery and dangerous is the subject that all major publishers and broadcasters retain the services of libel lawyers. At the first hint of trouble you are advised most strongly to get professional advice. In this chapter we can only give a broad outline of the major pitfalls with particular reference to the problems for television programme makers. For more detailed guidance the two most accessible handbooks for non-lawyers are probably *McNae's Essential Law for Journalists* published by Butterworth, 1995, and *Law and The Media* by Tom Crone published by Focal Press, 1995. The standard legal work is *Media Law* by Robertson and Nicol published by Penguin.

Defamation comes in two guises, slander and libel. Slander refers to verbal defamation and libel to the published form. In law utterances made during a radio or television programme or delivered on the stage have been effectively published and therefore come under the heading of libel. This of course raises peculiar problems for live discussion programmes particularly those using the device of the 'phone-in'.

Some broadcasters now resort to the technological solution of building in a delay which allows several seconds between the uttering of the words and their subsequent re-broadcast and gives a presenter time to hit a 'panic button' and cut off any obviously libellous material. This might keep most defamatory contributions off the air but presenters and directors are not lawyers, a slanderous remark is not always obvious at the time and the most spectacular libels are as likely to drop from the lips of a distinguished public figure as from a deranged member of the public.

The heat of the moment is no defence in law as London

Weekend Television discovered in 1985 when their football commentator Jimmy Greaves let slip a remark that a referee was 'trying to get his name in history before he retired' in the context of a disputed foul. The referee sued and won substantial damages and an apology on the grounds that his professional standing was brought into disrepute.

As will be seen the costs for all parties in conducting a libel action is so enormous that prosecuting the individual who utters the libel is usually not a profitable option. But the broadcaster who publishes it might be seen as fair game. The only way suggested for the broadcaster to mitigate libel is to make an immediate dissociation from the comments involved and subsequently a fulsome apology to the aggrieved party. If possible, discussion programmes should aspire to a balance so that an immediate riposte is possible. The offer of a right to reply in a later broadcast may also avert legal consequences, and as described in the following chapter, there are other formal means of seeking redress. But from the issue of the first solicitor's letter to the final settlement both parties are committed to a process which may last years rather than months, which may bankrupt either or both of them and where the only sure-fire winners are the lawyers: there is no legal aid in civil actions for libel.

To prove libel the plaintiff has to show:

- the remarks actually are defamatory;
- the statement could reasonably be taken to refer to him- or herself by a third party;
- the words have a damaging effect upon his or her reputation.

These conditions are rarely a problem for the plaintiff since libel law turns the usual assumptions of English law on their head. It is assumed that if the plaintiff thinks that a comment is defamatory then it likely is so and it is not necessary to prove that the words were deliberate or actually harm the plaintiff's reputation, merely that they 'tend' to do so. It is assumed that if a defamatory remark is made that intent is implied. In other words the defendant is effectively presumed guilty and has to prove his or her innocence.

The victim of a libel need not be named, merely identifiable. The newspaper tactic of heavily alluding to a supposed wrong doer without actually naming names is a dangerous one and is often used in an attempt to flush out the victim. But if the implied accusations turn out to be unproved the penalties can be heavy.

For example in 1987 the *Mail on Sunday* alleged that the log of the submarine which sank the Argentine cruiser *Belgrano* had been stolen by an un-named former officer currently living in the West Indies. Narendra Sethia who fitted the description argued that friends and relatives as well as former naval colleagues would take it to refer to him. An out-of-court settlement of £120 000 was agreed.

There are times though where a libel action will fail on the grounds that remarks are harmful but not damaging to the reputation. For example it may be professionally harmful to a businessman to say, wrongly, that he has taken retirement or is unwell but it would not be counted as defamatory. But it would be defamatory as well as harmful to say that he is financially insolvent or that the disease is a sexually transmitted one.

A statement is deemed to be libellous if:

- the plaintiff has been exposed to hatred, ridicule or contempt;
- it has caused the plaintiff to be shunned or avoided;
- it lowers his or her esteem in the eyes of right thinking members of society;
- it disparages him or her in a profession, office or trade.

And here of course is the rub, for who can define a 'right thinking member of society' any longer? It has been pointed out that in Edwardian times an allegation that a young woman had spent a holiday abroad unchaperoned with a boy friend would have been highly defamatory, whereas in contemporary society it would be hard to prove that her esteem was in any way lowered or she was in consequence likely to be shunned.

In England, though not in Scotland, libel cases are held before juries who also fix the amount of damages. Finding two sets of 12 'right thinking members of society' who would come to the same conclusions is very unlikely. A judge awarding damages for a physical injury has a whole set of precedents and guidelines based on the grievousness of the disability and its effect on the financial prospects of the victim. A jury trying to adjudicate on the price to put on damaged reputation or wounded vanity operates in the dark. Judgements are subjective. Libel cases have come to look less and less like processes of law and more and more like games of poker.

A classic example of the contemporary dilemma has been the 1992 case of the Australian entertainer Jason Donovan and the teen magazine *The Face*. During an interview in which he went into detail about his sexual athleticism it was implied that his tastes included homosexuality. Donovan sued on the grounds that he had denied being gay on previous occasions and that therefore was made to appear a hypocrite. The astonishing award by the jury of £200 000 damages caused uproar and the award would almost certainly have gone to appeal and been reduced. The award would have ruined *The Face,* one of the leading magazines read by his fans and courted by pop celebrities for publicity. More serious for Donovan there was outrage among gays at the suggestion that being called a homosexual was in any way defamatory. Donovan effectively climbed down, waived the damages, and issued a statement agreeing that there was nothing wrong in being gay.

The other slippery concept is that of being disparaged in a trade or profession. Many actions can result from wounded pride as much as damage. This can create problems for critical review. A spectacular case was that of the actress Charlotte Cornwell who in 1985 sued the *People* and its television critic Nina Myskow over a review of a television role which included the remarks 'Her bum's too big, she can't sing, she can't act and she has the sort of stage presence that jams lavatories.' The defendants claimed that this was robust comment rather than allegations of fact and therefore not actionable. The jury disagreed and awarded £10 000 damages.

The defendants successfully appealed on a technicality leaving Ms Cornwell to pursue a retrial in which a second jury awarded £11 500. Unfortunately she was left with the bill for the litigation which left her probably £50 000 out of pocket and the review in question is now immortalised in each law book on the subject.

The astronomic damages awarded by English juries in recent times have become legendary. Most of the more spectacular cases have involved the tabloid press but broadcasters and even small trade publications have borne the brunt of the irrationality of the system. In 1987 an ex-Navy intelligence agent was awarded £450 000 for a libel in a Greek language news sheet with a UK circulation of under 50; in the same year the writer Geoffrey Archer was awarded £500 000 against the *Star* newspaper. In 1989 the *Mail on Sunday* lost £470 000 for allegations about repackaging out-of-date food, and in 1988 the tiny trade journal *Stationery Trade News* had to pay £300 000 for an article about counterfeit trade names on envelopes. In 1990 the wife of 'The Yorkshire Ripper' was initially awarded £600 000 against *Private Eye*. Although, since

1990, it has been possible to appeal for a reduction of unreasonable damages there have been, at the time of writing, only three such cases and juries seem unabashed. In 1994 a jury made an astonishing award of £1.5 million to a firm of yacht designers and its directors over an unfavourable review of a prototype boat which had been greatly hyped by the firm's own publicity. And in the previous year Lord Aldington, the Conservative politician, was also awarded £1.5 million for allegations made in a pamphlet by the historian Count Tolstoy. Since neither Tolstoy nor a co-defendant had any money the award was a particularly ridiculous one. But it has resulted in an appeal first to the European Commission and then to the European Court. The first upheld the appeal on the grounds that the award was quite disproportionate to any harm done to Aldington's reputation, the second is still reserving judgement at the time of writing on the plea that English juries are so arbitrary and so ill instructed that their judgements could not be described as 'prescribed by law' according to the European Convention on Human Rights. In other words it is alleged that libel juries behave like kangaroo courts in the Old West.

Television has fared no better. Whereas some newspapers can cynically calculate that their eventual losses may be offset by increased circulation during a particularly juicy case, there is no such consolation for broadcasters. There is therefore a temptation for them to cut and run and settle out of court, in which case the plaintiff wins the poker game straight away. In 1985 the BBC was sued over allegations of medical professional misconduct on the 'That's Life' consumer programme. After fighting the case for 87 days the BBC threw in its hand and settled out of court for £75 000 damages. In the meantime its legal costs had soared to over £1 million. In 1994, in a not dissimilar medical case, a drugs company was awarded £60 000 against the BBC by a judge sitting without a jury over a 'Panorama' programme, 'The Halcion Nightmare'. Despite the comparatively modest award the BBC also was landed with costs estimated to be about £1.5 million.

There is no redress if the allegations are subsequently proved to be justified. In 1959 the pianist Liberace successfully sued the *Daily Mirror* over remarks which implied his homosexuality. He subsequently became involved in a US palimony case against his companion/chauffeur and died of AIDS. In a reprise of this case in 1982 the footballer Justin Fashanu settled with the *People* for substantial damages out of court after reports about his sexuality. He subsequently 'came out' and admitted he was gay.

Defences

There are only five defences against a charge of libel:

- The statement is true.
- The comment is fair.
- The circumstances were privileged.
- There has already been 'accord and satisfaction' between the parties.
- The libel was unintentional.

It is no defence to claim that a defamatory statement was in the public interest if that statement cannot be proven in court. Public interest can be claimed as a defence only in circumstances defined as covered by privilege. Neither is it a defence in law to have mitigated a libel by offering an apology and a right to reply. As a tactic it may smooth ruffled feathers, but unless formally accepted as recompense under 'accord and satisfaction' the offer might even be taken by the court for an admission of guilt.

Truth

The defence has to prove truth 'on the balance of probabilities'. This may not be as easy as it would appear. For example in 1988 the Liverpool radio station Radio City had to pay £350 000 over allegations made in a consumer discussion show about the activities of a travel firm run by a couple from their home. The broadcast claimed that the proprietors made promises that could not be kept and was indifferent to the suffering of customers.

The firm did not try to dispute the allegations of particular clients, merely the presumption of the programme that this behaviour was habitual. The radio station produced 19 witnesses whose holidays had been ruined. The company produced 21 who had no complaints. The company won. Travel companies seem to be a particular problem in other ways as described below.

Fair comment

There is a plea of public interest that an apparently defamatory comment was made in good faith, without malice and on a matter of public interest. The trap is that it is necessary to distinguish between the alleged facts and the comment on them. If the facts cannot be shown to be true then the comment based on them cannot be justified. Comment by itself cannot be either true or false by its nature and so need not be proven. Whether comment is in itself fair or not is a matter of opinion and the right to comment is the basic right to free speech. The main requisite is to prove that the opinions expressed are honestly held and not motivated by malice. But as the Charlotte Cornwell case illustrates, dividing fact from comment and honest criticism from malice is not straightforward.

Privilege

The law recognises certain defined areas where otherwise defamatory statements may be made and published without risk. Privilege is either absolute or conditional. Absolute privilege is restricted to the reporting of parliamentary debates and parliamentary committees and of the courts. Although such reporting remains a minefield it is at least a well charted one and journalists must be briefed in the rules. As parliamentary and court reporting is so specialised the programme maker should refer to the authors noted above.

Qualified privilege enables the coverage of a whole range of public meetings and statements ranging from reports on local government meetings and police statements to almost every kind of lawful meeting to discuss matters of public interest from international conferences to general meetings of public companies. Some statements, if defamatory, may require the publisher to offer the offended parties the right to explanation or contradiction, others are almost as well priveleged as those made in Parliament. The conditions are very precisely defined in the schedule to the 1952 Defamation Act.

The rub is that the world of 1952 was a very different one to the one we now live in. In 1993 the *Western Morning Press* was sued by a doctor for publishing remarks made by the chairman of a National Health Service Trust. The sequence of events was that a number of disaffected doctors had appeared on a local television programme to complain that staff shortages put patients' lives at risk. The newspaper interviewed the chairman who made defamatory remarks about the consultant in charge. The doctor subsequently sued both the chairman and the newspaper. One of the allegations was that two patients had needlessly died and that this was a matter of public concern covered by reporting privilege. Had the events occurred before 1990 when the hospital was governed by a publicly accountable Regional Health Authority the newspaper would have had statutory privilege in reporting statements put out by the governing body. The new trusts are not covered by the 1952 Act.

The implications for privileged reporting are significant. During the 1980s and 1990s the government has indulged in an orgy of privatisation of previously public bodies and devolution of powers from local government control to various trusts and quangos. The justification of privileged reporting in the public interest seems to becoming very limited indeed.

Accord and satisfaction

This is the procedure described above, commonly resorted to by broadcasters to avoid court proceedings. It might be best described as strategic grovelling, with the aim of agreeing to publish a correction or retraction and an apology. Correspondence between the parties should always be headed by the legal get-out phrase 'without prejudice' meaning 'off the record' until a formal agreement is reached preferably in the shape of a waiver by the aggrieved party of any further claims for damages.

Unintentional defamation

So far, the cases referred to will be the main concern of news and current affairs style programmes and in particular their journalists and editors. But when we enter the realm of unintentional defamation then all kinds of programme makers may find themselves at risk.

The most often quoted case is that of Artemus Jones. In 1910 the *Sunday Chronicle* published a humorous report on English tourists travelling to Dieppe for fun and games. One of the imaginary types portrayed was Artemus Jones travelling with a lady 'not his wife, you know, rather one of the other'.

Unhappily there existed, against all likelihood, a real Artemus Jones and he happened to be a solicitor. Despite a complete lack of connection with anything in the piece, he successfully sued for libel.

History repeated itself in 1940 when Harold Newstead of Camberwell successfully sued *Express Newspapers* for a report about 'Harold Newstead a Camberwell man sent to prison for nine months for bigamy'. Although the newspaper had been unaware of the existence of two Harold Newsteads the court found against the paper on the grounds that the bigamous one was not identified clearly enough.

It is to avoid this mistake that so many reports build in apparently extraneous descriptive material such as 'Rosie Bliggins mother of three living at Steptoe Cuttings Basingstoke replying to accusations of keeping a disorderly house said ...'.

Under the 1952 Act it is possible to plead that a libel took place through accident and not through carelessness, in other words blaming it on Murphy's Law. For this defence to succeed the defendant must have made a suitably prominent apology and correction of the mistake. It must be demonstrated that no libel was intended and there was no awareness that the defamation could ever have applied to a third party. Above all, and this is most significant in a television context, it must be clear that every reasonable precaution had been taken in advance. The Newstead case would probably have failed even if this defence had been available at the time. It would not have been unreasonable for a newspaper to have checked on the existence of a second Harold Newstead living in the same borough. It was carelessness not to have clearly identified the bigamous one.

Pictures as well as words may be defamatory

Every newspaper editor dreads the occasion where a photographer or researcher provides pictures of the wrong school or the wrong vicar for a story, but television with its reliance on pictures is particularly exposed. Topical programmes particularly rely upon 'wall-paper shots' as general background to essentially non-visual stories, and these shots may be hurriedly shot or obtained from other agencies.

In one case a story about police corruption was illustrated by the exterior of a police station with a man walking through shot. The man in question turned out to be an identifiable CID officer unconnected with the allegations. He sued Granada Television and was awarded £20 000.

Music may be libellous

One Commonwealth Prime Minister was not well pleased to watch a recording in which his arrival was accompanied by a dubbed sound track. The melody in question was that of the ballad 'Olé I Am The Bandit'. In this particular Far Eastern country aggrieved politicians have more direct ways of seeking redress than the laws of libel. But a director can equally come unstuck in the UK. In one instance a holiday programme accompanied a damning report on holiday accommodation with the theme music from a current drama series 'Colditz'. The juxtaposition of music and pictures for comic or satirical purposes is a common trick but in this case the travel company was not amused and an out-of-court settlement was made.

Headteachers of schools are particularly prickly. It is established that stories of bullying, abuse or simply poor teaching reflect upon the headteacher concerned and are liable to be defamatory. The truth of such stories is frequently hard to prove in court even when they are common knowledge, since the witnesses are frequently children and the protesters are the parents who are in effect relaying hearsay. But woe betide the programme maker who uses shots of school buildings or children in identifiable uniforms for anything but the most precise illustrative purposes.

There has been a great deal of concern about the use of dramatic reconstruction as a way round some of these problems. Unfortunately the question of identification is frequently the key issue in a criminal trial and even if a director resorts to the tricks of shooting actors from behind, or in silhouette, or in disguise, it is impossible to eliminate all details of clothing, voice or stature and body language. The vivid impressions of a television reconstruction may become clearer and more memorable in the mind of a witness than a real but muddled recollection.

Reconstructions must always be clearly labelled reconstruction on the screen and are only completely safe in illustrating cases which have already passed the full procedures of trial, conviction and appeal. Even then ethical as well as legal questions arise.

No two witnesses will ever tell an identical story even when recounting apparently obvious events. Film buffs will recall the classic Japanese film *Rashomon* in which the story of a rape and murder is seen through the eyes of each of the protagonists. They recount completely different stories leaving the audience to decide which one of them (or maybe all of them), tells the truth.

So the director has to pick carefully which version to base a dramatisation upon. Hence the importance of not showing identifiable faces, car registration plates or similar items in reconstructions of criminal acts. The consequences of too imaginative a dramatisation may be proceedings for contempt of court.

Negative checks

The best protection for all programme makers whether working in factual programmes, entertainment or drama is to routinely follow a procedure known as negative checking. This avoids embarrassment as well as providing the defence of having taken all reasonable care if the worst comes to the worst.

Names

Remember Artemus Jones. There may be no batty vicar called Pritchard in a village called Fidget Monochrome but it pays to check the clergy register and a gazetteer of place names just in case.

Addresses

Do not use real or possibly real addresses or street names particularly if a town is either named or easily recognisable. Even if the context flatters the occupants an a broadcast can trigger a spate of crank abusive or begging letters or unwelcome visits not to mention the ire of neighbours who are not entranced by the sudden notoriety of their street. Most towns have a gazetteer or an A to Z street directory.

Telephone numbers

Do not use real telephone numbers (unless you use your own and are willing to risk the consequences) and do not randomly invent fictitious ones. Non-operative numbers can be obtained from:

 British Telecom
Numbers Allocations
151 Shaftesbury Avenue
London WC2 HBA

Car number plates

It is an offence to possess a car with false number plates on the public highway but it is also frequently libellous or in contempt of court to show real numbers in a crime reconstruction. Hence the device of electronically blacking out registration numbers in drama reconstructions.

In a dramatic context it may be necessary to have a number plate showing an appropriate year of registration or district of origin. The audience will spot any fantastical invention. If a real car and registration is shown the prior permission of the owner must be asked.

To be on the safe side, non-active registration numbers may be supplied by:

 The Driving and Vehicle Licensing Centre
Swansea
Wales SA99 1AB

Brand names

In common parlance people often use specific brand names in a generic context. In other words all types of adhesive tape get described as Sellotape, ballpoint pens as Biros, vacuum cleaners as Hoovers, cola drinks as Coke and so on. This is particularly galling for marketing consultants and may be a problem for the director. It can lead to a complaint if an incorrect term is used in the context of a rival product. Even worse would be to use a clearly identifiable manufacture of goods in a pejorative manner. If the comic sketch revolves around a fridge full of rotting food or an exploding washing machine it is wise not to show any identifiable name or logo in shot.

Trade names and marks may be checked, for a fee, with:

The Trade Marks Registry
66–71 High Holborn
London WC1R 4TP

Companies

Since 1982 there has been no compulsory registration of small businesses other than limited liability companies. So it is very dangerous to invent a trade name for a shop or company without keeping in mind the case of the two Harold Newsteads.

Our old friends the travel firms are a good illustration. Most belong to one or more professional organisations but many do not. They exist in large numbers and come and go with considerable frequency, often in dubious circumstances leaving a trail of aggrieved holiday makers. They have the tedious habit of adopting names with the limited permutations of words like sun, sea, sky, tour, travel, world and globe.

Each time complaints about one company are reported, there are likely to be wails of protest from others bearing near identical names. So if you carelessly invent a firm called Skyworld, Sunglobe, Travelways, etc. there is more than a good chance that such a firm exists. Limited Liability Companies are kept on a database held by:

The Companies Registration Office
55 City Road
London EC1

Other identities

The director, journalist or researcher can come unstuck over a whole range of names in either a real or fictitious context. Prominent examples are the names of clinics and hospitals, ships, theatres, air companies and flight numbers, company directors, police officers (a litigious bunch), song titles, actors and musicians, ships, clergymen and members of professional or social groups such as doctors, officers in the armed forces, or members of the nobility. All of these can be checked through various gazettes and official lists available in any good reference library.

It is even possible to defame a racehorse if you use the name of an owner's treasured winner in the context of a doping scandal or a sketch about a broken-down nag. In this case the charge may be not for libel but for malicious falsehood.

If a production cannot deploy a researcher to conduct negative checks there are professional library services which will undertake the job. One such with particular experience is:

 BBC Data Services
Broadcasting House
Portland Place
London W1A 1AA

Malicious falsehood

The case of the unfairly maligned horse would most likely incur a charge of malicious falsehood. Cases of malicious falsehood are different from libel in that they are heard before a judge and not a jury and it is for the plaintiff to prove damage rather than the defendant to prove the truth of his statements. We are back on the familiar legal ground of innocent until proved guilty.

Actions for malicious falsehood are subject to legal aid and so are within the reach of those unable to contemplate the enormous sums needed to conduct libel proceedings.

Our horse would be a victim of a type of malicious falsehood known as slander of goods and the plaintiffs, presumably the owner and trainer, would have to prove that the falsehood incurred, or was likely to incur, financial loss. It would also be necessary to show that the offending material was published maliciously.

The concept of malice in legal parlance does not just imply a motivation of spite or dishonesty but can include any improper motive or just careless indifference to the consequences. If the court finds for the plaintiff it may be possible to go on to seek civil damages for the distress caused by the original case.

A landmark case in 1992 was that of a Buckingham Palace maid who wished to sue the *Today* newspaper over allegations that she had purloined personal letters belonging to Princess

Anne. As she could not afford to undertake an action for libel she was given leave to receive legal aid for an action for malicious falsehood. After loud protests the defendant's lawyers decided to settle out of court for £25 000. Whether this is welcomed as a way the ordinary person can circumvent the unreformed libel laws, or is to be deplored as another dangerous weapon for curbing the media, will have to be seen.

Confidentiality

Programme makers in the topical and documentary areas cannot work without research, and research regularly turns up information given in confidence. If this information is detrimental to the person who originally passed it to the programme maker ought to offer the party a chance for explanation or rebuttal. This ought to be a matter of professional ethics as well as strict adherence to the law of libel. Unfortunately such an offer is likely to send the aggrieved party hot foot to the courts to seek an injunction to prevent publication. There might also then be a demand that the source of the confidential material be identified and the material itself handed up to the court.

This dilemma is often thought of as the exclusive problem for the investigative reporter pursuing leaks and tip-offs about shady politicians and fraudulent business deals. This is no longer necessarily so. The law of confidentiality is being used increasingly to silence the media in subjects as different as medicine, industry, entertainment and even the Royal Family. It is described by Tom Crone in *Law and the Media* as a new 'boom area'.

In 1981 the writer who successfully challenged the old adage that there is no copyright in ideas did so by invoking the law for breach of confidence. He had given his ideas for the series subsequently called 'Rock Follies' in confidence and the television company had broken that confidence by offering the script to another writer.

A more familiar example is that of Schering Chemical versus Falkman in 1981. A television producer who also worked as a training consultant heard of a story concerning the drug Primados which was under suspicion of causing damage to unborn babies. Thames Television took up the story which it researched from sources which had been published already. Schering Chemicals were alerted about the programme and sought an injunction to stop the broadcast. The court upheld the drug company's case on the basis that the original idea had been obtained whilst the producer had been in the employ of the company and was therefore bound by confidence.

An injunction forbidding publication until both sides can argue the case in court, is normally enough to kill a story. An *ex parte* injunction, i.e. on behalf of only one of the parties, can be obtained with no more than a telephone call to the High Court. There is no requirement to notify the publisher until after the injunction has been granted and this may be done by no more than a last-minute telephone call. To get the injunction lifted the defendant has to apply for an *inter pares* hearing, i.e. one at which both parties are present to plead their cases, by which time the damage often is done.

For newspapers old news is no news. For a television documentary programme the lack of topicality may be less important but last minute re-scheduling may kill a programme off and injunctions can be imposed in perpetuity meaning that an expensive programme will have to be written off.

So the law of confidentiality, backed by penalties for contempt of court, is a cheaper and more immediate way of silencing the media than the unpredictable laws of libel.

The law assumes a degree of confidentiality between employer and employee even when no written contract exists. In fact employers in certain areas are increasingly aware of the force of the law and impose commitments to confidentiality. There have been numerous examples of whistle-blowing by disaffected employees in the National Health Service and the privatised public utilities within recent years; and it does not stop there.

In 1987 the television presenter Anne Diamond won an injunction to stop the *Sun* newspaper publishing a story about her domestic life on the grounds that the information had been leaked by her ex-nanny who had broken confidence.

In 1982 Robert Maxwell, who so successfully used the law to silence the rest of the media, discovered that the *Watford Observer* was about to publish a story that Sun Printers was losing money and was discussing redundancies. As Sun Printers was an important local employer the story was clearly in the public interest. Maxwell waited until the day on which the presses were to turn and then obtained an injunction forbidding publication on the grounds that the story originated in a leaked discussion document and was therefore confidential. Fortunately the newspaper had been alerted about the threat from Maxwell and prepared an alternative front page. A subsequent appeal led to the injunction being overturned. The *Watford Observer* had foiled the plan to wipe out a complete edition and Maxwell had silenced his critic only temporarily, but the paper was still left with a sizeable legal bill.

In 1990 Maxwell again sought an injunction, this time unsuccessfully. In that same year there appeared two biographies, one sycophantic and the other critical. In the case of the latter, Maxwell sought to have the book withdrawn on the grounds that information in it had been obtained from someone who used to work as one of his secretaries.

The same Robert Maxwell also used injunctions for breach of confidence by his employees not merely to suppress information but to prevent reporting that an injunction existed. In other words he persuaded the judge that public knowledge of an injunction's existence would be as harmful to him as allowing the publication of the offending material. It would be as if the case had never existed. An injunction applying to one part of the media applies to all and it is common practice to notify all newspaper editors as soon as one has been granted. The gagging ought then to be complete.

In 1992 the leader of the Liberal Democrats, Paddy Ashdown, became aware that confidential material had mysteriously been removed from his solicitor's office. It revealed evidence of an extra-marital affair and was about to be made public by the *News of the World*. He sought and obtained a comprehensive gagging injunction à la Robert Maxwell. Unfortunately he forgot that an injunction granted by the English courts does not apply in the Scottish ones. The *Scotsman* newspaper published all the details and the cat was out of the bag.

In 1994 the lottery company Camelot tried to enforce an injunction against the press which had successfully identified the winner of the jackpot despite their assurances of anonymity. In this case the newspapers won on the grounds that even if they had resorted to material confidential to Camelot, the identity of the winner was already common knowledge in his family, workplace and home town.

In 1993 breach of confidence took a new turn when the Princess of Wales was photographed exercising at a London health club with a hidden camera set up by the proprietor. Hitherto, breach of confidence had been taken to concern verbal or written information rather than photographs. The proprietors had, however, made an undertaking to respect the privacy of the Princess. The *Daily Mirror* published pictures on two successive days and promised more. The Princess obtained an interim injunction to prevent any further publication and then sued for damages. The *Mirror* maintained that there was no secret about the attendance of the Princess at the health club and that she would have been clearly visible to the public through a window. In the end both the proprietor and *Mirror* apologised and there was a settlement out of court. As the matter never came to court it is impossible to say whether this extension of the law of confidentiality to encompass matters of personal privacy would have stood up.

There are four main defences against an action over confidentiality:

- The information is already available in the public domain. This was pleaded unsuccessfully in the Primodos case.
- The owner of the information has consented to publication. If the vicar has expressed some bizarre views in his church magazine, he cannot then claim breach of confidence if a parishioner sends them to a national tabloid.
- The information discloses iniquity. There can be no confidentiality in material which conceals criminality. The trouble with this defence is that it is difficult to establish in the hurried procedure of a injunction. It can be argued that the first priority of the journalist is to place such matters in the hands of the police rather than seek publication or broadcast.
- Disclosure is in the public interest. The courts try to keep a balance between the need to maintain confidentiality and the need for the public to be informed in matters of common interest. The problem lies in being able to distinguish between that which is in the public interest and that which is simply interesting to the public. The cult of the Church of Scientology has tried unsuccessfully and repeatedly to claim breach of confidence to prevent publication of its texts. The English courts which obviously take a dim view of Scientology have repeatedly rejected their claims on the grounds that the public have a right to be informed about what the sect is up to. In this case confidentiality is being used as an alternative to copyright law. At the time of writing the Scientologists are attempting to injunct the publication of their material over the Internet. New technology is presenting some new dilemmas to the law.

As we have seen the law of confidentiality has been used as a blunt instrument where otherwise procedures for things as diverse as libel and copyright might seem more appropriate. But the most celebrated use or misuse of the law has been its application by the government as an alternative to the Official Secrets Act.

Two great causes célèbres of the late 1980s were the Spycatcher Affair and the Zircon Affair. They are related.

In 1985 an ex-secret service officer living in Australia proposed to publish his memoirs, entitled *Spycatcher*, and purporting to reveal a number of past dirty tricks by the security services. These included a plot to destabilise the Labour government of Harold Wilson and involvement in burglary and illegal bugging. An attempt to prevent publication in the Australian courts failed. In the English courts the defence attempted to prove that the books revealed iniquity. The injunction was upheld, however, on the grounds that government security officers were bound by a lifetime duty of confidentiality.

There then followed almost four years of high farce. The book was at various stages banned, serialised, printed in Ireland, smuggled into England in bulk to become a sort of English samidzat best seller and finally wearily accepted by the Court of Appeal on the grounds that the cat was out of the bag. The government was (uniquely perhaps) not amused and lashed out at other suspected breaches of confidentiality.

In 1987 an injunction was sought against BBC Radio 4 to prevent it publishing a programme, 'My Country Right or Wrong', about the security services. It named names and used once-confidential information. But the court deemed it no defence that the same material had already been published and the identities of the authors were common knowledge. Ironically the subject matter had already been passed by the, then, D notice committee of the government itself.

In the same year the government reverted to the sledgehammer of the Official Secrets Act to prevent the transmission of the television series 'The Secret Society' which alleged that Parliament had been deceived about the expenditure of £500 million on a secret spy satellite called Zircon. Police raided the home of the journalist Duncan Campbell as well as those of the *New Statesman* which intended to publish the substance of the allegations. The Scottish police also raided the offices of BBC Scotland and removed the programme files. Campbell was ordered to hand over any documents obtained from ex-employees of the signals intelligence centre GCHQ (Government Communication Headquarters) and to reveal his sources.

The ensuing uproar about an apparent shift towards a police state led to a new Official Secrets Act in 1990 and a promise in 1992 to sweep away 'the cobwebs of secrecy' though so far this seems to amount to little more than the right to publish the identity of the head of MI5. In the meantime there is pressure for a formal Bill of Rights and a Freedom of Information Act similar to that of the USA. It is an increasingly noted illogically that material jealously protected as confidential in the UK is at the same time freely obtainable from the USA over the Internet. Such matters are not just political but affect in particular evidence about food manufacturers and drugs companies. The Primados prosecution was brought in England because although the evidence was already published in the USA no prosecution would have succeeded there.

The 1990 Official Secrets Act applies to secret information covered by security, intelligence, defence, international relations, confidential material entrusted to other states and inter- national organisations, and officially sanctioned phone tapping and interception of communications. In most, but not all cases the prosecution will have to prove that the revelation of confidential material has been harmful to the security of the state.

Again much of this would appear to concern newspaper journalists and news programmes more than the ordinary programme maker. There are, however, broad implications for everyone. It has been noted how in confidentiality cases the courts can insist on the handing up of source material and how the government used legal means to raid the offices of both broadcasters and journals.

The police have used additional powers to oblige television broadcasters to hand over their material. In 1988 both BBC and ITV cameramen were witnesses to the horrific lynching of two British soldiers by an IRA mob. The police successfully demanded the handing over of all footage as a means to identifying the murderers which under Northern Irish laws of the time they were entitled to do. The broadcasters attempted to defend their retention of unbroadcast rushes on the grounds that in future their crews would be seen as government agents and that their future safety and ability to report events would be compromised.

In 1990 numerous television and film crews were present at the anti-poll tax riots in Whitehall and Trafalgar Square. Indeed on this occasion many of those on the demonstrators side had video cameras and much later Channel 4 was able to transmit a programme showing the demonstrations from the other side and refuting the accepted police version of events. But in the immediate aftermath of the riots a grand total of 29 news-gathering organisations were obliged by the police under the Police and Criminal Evidence Act to hand over all their footage, transmitted or not, for the identification of offenders. The story was repeated after the violent demonstrations against the Criminal Justice and Public Order Act in 1994.

Regardless of the legal or ethical arguments the implications are clear. The police and other official agencies already use video cameras on a regular basis quite openly. The huge increase in the numbers of accredited crews as well as freelance video paparazzi and enthusiastic amateurs is obvious. One of the strengths of television reporting has been a general public assumption, misguided, that crews were in some way trustworthy, independent and impartial in the issues they were filming. If footage is to be available on request to the police, the future is not very bright for the adventurous journalist or documentary maker.

Sources of information

All journalists and researchers come across the problem that information they uncover is frequently confidential in nature and that a revelation of the source may have dire consequences for the originator of the leaked information.

This is not to say that institutions – even cabinet ministers and Buckingham Palace – are not averse to deliberately leaking information which might be embarrassing if disseminated as an official statement.

There is a long history of battles between journalists and the government and the courts over the protection of sources. Generally the matter at issue has been one of national security but not always so.

There is no statutory right for a journalist to refuse to name his or her sources. If he or she does so, both a fine and imprisonment for Contempt of Court are possible. Two recent cases illustrate the point.

In 1992 an independent production company Box Productions and Channel 4 Television were fined £75 000 for contempt for refusing to reveal the source of information about the role of the police in death squads during the Ulster troubles. Naturally the Royal Ulster Constabulary denied the allegations. The Director of Public Prosecutions demanded a seizure of assets, which would in essence have caused the closure of Channel 4 television. The television company pleaded the unreasonableness of asking it to hand over incriminating evidence to the very people being accused, namely the Royal Ulster Constabulary. The judge only settled for the lesser penalty by accepting the basic responsibility of the defendants' motives but observed that the producers had landed themselves in court through giving their informants an unqualified assurance of confidentiality. This, they were in no position to do.

An apparently more obscure case may have more momentous consequences.

In 1989 Bill Goodwin, a trainee reporter working on a trade magazine, *The Engineer*, obtained information that a firm, Tetra Ltd, was in financial difficulties. *The Engineer* is hardly a popular tabloid and such stories are normal copy for trade journals. The reporter responsibly telephoned the firm prior to publication for confirmation. The firm realised that the information could only have come from a missing copy of their business plan and obtained an injunction under the law of confidentiality. The judge ordered the reporter to reveal the source of his information but he refused and was fined £5 000. The National Union of Journalists took up the case, which went on appeal to the House of Lords. The Lords found that, whatever the merits of the case, a journalist has no right to unqualified privilege and cannot put himself above the law.

However, the NUJ then took the case to the European Commission for Human Rights. The Commission found that the media would be unable to perform their democratic duties if compelled to reveal their sources and the court order against the reporter in this case violated his human right. If the reporter's information in *The Engineer* came from confidential sources then so does most of the information finding its way into a free press. In 1995 the case went on to the European Court.

In April 1996 the European Court not only ruled in favour of Goodwin but gave him the right to sue for compensation. Goodwin had never sought damages on the grounds that fighting for justice was part of the job of being a journalist.

The court ruled that only exceptional circumstances, the prevention of a crime or danger to life and limb should justify a journalist breaking his work. The fine imposed on Mr Goodwin was not 'necessary in a democratic society'. It was wrong of the British courts to cause someone 'mental anguish and anxiety of being threatened with imprisonment for obeying conscience and ethical duties'. Presumably now the Contempt of Court Act will have to be modified to bring it into line with the European ruling.

15

SEX, VIOLENCE, BLASPHEMY, RACE, OBSCENITY, CENSORSHIP AND ALL THAT

A visitor to Britain seeing the bombardment of criticism of television in the popular press and on radio phone-in programmes might conclude that our television is an unending cesspit of pornography, violence and foul-mouthed abuse.

Politicians, particularly those of the party in power, regularly whip themselves into a froth over the supposed gross bias and irresponsibility of television programmes and the need for their makers to be curbed. At the same time there exists a comforting perception that the British enjoy freedoms of speech and conduct denied to lesser democracies.

The reality is quite the reverse. Television of all types in the UK is subject to controls and constraints both formal and informal which are unlike anything practised by other countries of the EU with the possible exception of the Republic of Ireland. The confusing and unwieldy structures for regulation and control simply represent successive waves of reaction by governments against perceived threats to national morals, culture and political stability (or to put ir another way, their chance of being re-elected). They also reflect the national confusion over standards of taste and decency. The BBC issues guidelines to producers which define the problem but consistently fail to get us any nearer to a solution.

The borderline between taste and decency is narrow. One useful distinction is to regard decency as a fundamental value while taste is a matter of manners. What is acceptable at one time and in one set of circumstances may not be in another. Accordingly Parliament has legislated for a set of statutory bodies to adjudicate on such matters and impose standards, in some cases backed by the force of law. The press is controlled by the Obscene Publications Act 1959 but radio and television transmissions are specifically not covered. Films and videotapes are. All that needs be said is that if the law is an ass, when it comes to matters of regulating public taste and morals it wears very long ears indeed.

The British Board of Film Classification

This body, originally the Board of Film Censors, was set up by the film industry itself in 1912 to overcome the complications which arose when films had to be previewed and passed as decent by the watch committee of each and every local government council in turn. The idea was to set up a board of censors with no greater powers than those of persuasion, whose independence and integrity was so evident that local authorities would defer to its judgements automatically. The board set the first nationally recognised standards for taste and decency.

To this day, however, the right to ban or censor the contents of a film remains with the local authority responsible for licensing the cinemas within its jurisdiction. Although each can, in theory, establish its own criteria the majority accept a Home Office set of model conditions for granting a licence.

- No film apart from newsreels will be shown without a BBFC certificate of classification.
- Young people shall be excluded from films the BBFC deems unsuitable for them.
- No film shall be exhibited if the licensing authority gives written notice prohibiting it.
- Films shall exhibit their classification on screen before the showing and in any publicity at the entrance to the cinema.
- Publicity material shall not display material not in the film as shown.
- Advertisements are subject to the same conditions as other films.

The London boroughs have gone a step further and banned films which might:

- Encourage or incite crime.
- Lead to disorder.
- Stir up hatred on grounds of colour, race, ethnic or national origins, sexual orientation or sex.
- Promote sexual humiliation or degradation or violence towards women.

- Tend to deprave and corrupt persons who see it.
- Contain a grossly indecent performance outraging the standards of public decency.

Some of these conditions do no more than re-state the position in common law but others go far beyond this and the Board has the obligation to adjudicate. The board receives no subsidy from the film industry or government and pays its way by charging fees for viewing films. At least two examiners must be present to view each film and if there are to be cuts these must be agreed by both of them. Producers have the right to receive notice of requested alterations in writing and may appeal and discuss alternatives. Most problems can be resolved by altering the classification of a film but as no producer of a blockbuster would want to see his or her work restricted to the top shelf of a sex shop, an accommodation can usually be found. As the board has no statutory powers it is still open to the producers to appeal directly to a local authority for a licence and a local authority might still impose a local ban if it disagrees with the leniency of the BBFC.

In the 1950s and 1960s, productions outlawed throughout the provinces were frequently allowed public showings in London cinemas. A recent cause case was the banning in some towns of *Monty Python's Life of Brian* on grounds of blasphemy.

The various classifications are:

U	Universal and suitable for all.
Uc	Particularly suitable for children.
PG	Parental guidance recommended but suitable for general viewing.
12	Suitable only for persons aged 12 or over.
15	Suitable only for those aged 15 or over.
18	Suitable only for those aged 18 or over.
R18	Restricted to adults and to be shown only in licensed sex shops or cinemas.

Which is all very well except it implies that a cinema manager can distinguish between a 14 and a 15 year old and makes some fairly breathtaking assumptions about the exercise of parental guidance. It ignores, of course, the fact that its carefully categorised films are available on television and may be hired from the neighbourhood video shop.

In 1984 the government, in an effort to shut the door on the technological stable, passed the Video Recordings Act which extended the role of the BBFC to videotapes. In this case the board has statutory powers enforceable by trading standards officers. Offensive uncertificated videos can be seized and their distributors prosecuted. The Criminal Justice Act of 1991 further endorses the statutory powers of the board to ban offensive material. The satellite channel BSkyB has requested that productions shown on its sub-scription channels be certificated by the board before transmission.

Of course such is the flood of videos produced – corporate, advertising, training, musical or indeed graphic video games – that it would take an army of censors to try to certificate the lot of them. It is therefore left to the programme makers to decide whether their production is so innocuous that classification is not necessary. None the less retail outlets may be very cautious about selling tapes without the BBFC seal of approval.

Where the board does make a decision it is legally binding though there is a Video Appeals Committee to consider objections. So the video maker may assume exemption unless his or her work includes one of the following:

- Human sexual activity or force associated with such activity.
- Mutilation, torture or gross violence towards humans or animal.
- Human genital organs or urinary or excretory functions.
- Techniques likely to be useful in the commission of offences.

A problem is that some types of video, for example pop music promotion tapes, contain images of blatant sex and violence, some video games have both sadistic and erotic content and even instructional tapes contain fairly clear information on how to break into a car, make explosives or grow marijuana. Material of gruesomely sadistic nature can be packaged as historical archive productions and of course soft porn is everywhere available under the guise of sex education.

Aware that the problems are potentially increasing, the industry has set up its own voluntary regulatory body which will suggest age suitability criteria for videos and games which apparently do not require BBFC certification. The European Software Publishers Association has organised the system which is administered in the UK by the Video Standards Council.

In 1995 for the first time in over 70 years the board was challenged. The spoof erotic sleaze epic *Bare Behind Bars* made by Redemption Films was refused a classification. The decision was upheld by the Video Appeals Committee. Redemption Films has been given leave to appeal against the decision on the grounds that the BBFC has been neither fair nor consistent and they are requesting a judicial review of the certification procedures. This should lead to a testing of the controversial parts of the Criminal Justice Act as applied to censorship. What will make fascinating reading will be if this or a similar appeal results in an appeal to the European Commission of Human Rights. Apart from videos dealing in acts which are themselves criminal such as child pornography and bestiality for which the law provides stringent punishments, most types of material in question are freely available and even broadcast in Europe and North America.

The addresses of the two standards bodies are:

The British Board of Film Classification
3 Soho Square
London W1V 5DE

The Video Standards Council
Research House
Fraser Road
Perivale
London UB6 7AQ

The Broadcasting Complaints Committee

The Broadcasting Complaints Committee (BCC) was set up by the Broadcasting Act 1981. Its brief is to adjudicate on complaints of unjust treatment in programmes and infringements of privacy in either the programmes themselves or during their preparation. It was not set up to adjudicate on matters of taste. It may only adjudicate on programmes after they have been broadcast and it is not concerned with the conduct in general of either broadcasters or companies.

It is specifically excluded from hearing complaints about:

- sex or violence;
- bad language;
- programme scheduling;
- background music.

It will only hear complaints from those with a direct interest in the programmes. General complaints from the public are not within its remit.

If the BCC takes up a grievance it may demand to see the programme in question and investigate the grounds for complaint. If it finds against the programme makers its sanction is to demand that its findings be published prominently in print or on air. It currently adjudicates on around one thousand complaints a year, the overwhelming majority of which are rejected.

In the light of other restrictions on broadcasters this sounds fairly minor, but at the time there was outrage that the government was interfering with the independence of the governors of the BBC and the Independent Broadcasting Authority. The then Director General of the BBC described the BCC as 'a pain in the neck'.

The Broadcasting Standards Council

There was considerably more uproar at the Broadcasting Act 1990 which set up a second body, the Broadcasting Standards Council (BSC). The BSC is charged specifically to watch over the portrayal of sex and violence and matters of taste and decency. The BSC was set up at a time when the Prime Minister was talking of the BBC being 'out of control' and there were signs of paranoia in political circles. The broadcasters themselves talked in terms of a new inquisition and police state censorship. In the event the BSC does little more than restate the existing voluntary codes of the BBC, the Independent Television Authority and the Radio Authority.

If a member of the public wishes to complain he or she must do so within two months of transmission for television or three weeks for radio. The Council may demand a copy of the programme in question and summon a hearing in which both the complainant and the broadcasters are present. If it finds against the company the BSC may demand that its findings be published in the press and on air at the expense of the company concerned.

The Council commissions and publishes some very interesting research work and also issues a monthly résumé of complaints received and its findings. It also has drawn up its own model code of voluntary practice for programme makers which looks the same as every other voluntary code of practice. The BSC is not allowed to adjudicate on matters of accuracy in factual programmes.

As far as the two main networks have been concerned, the BSC has been little more than a harmless quango and a safety valve for vocal protest groups.

However, its remit includes all broadcasts which includes cable and satellite. The scale of its remit has therefore suddenly exploded and it is cable and satellite which is causing most of today's complaints and deliberations.

According to the Broadcasting Bill passing through Parliament in 1996 the two bodies are to be amalgamated into a new Broadcasting Standards Council from the auspicious date of 1 April 1997. The new body promises an inaugural report on fairness in programmes, an area not dealt with by either of the two previous bodies.

Broadcasting Complaints Committee/Broadcasting Standards Council
7 The Sanctuary
London SWAP 3JS

The Independent Television Commission

The Broadcasting Act 1990 established the Independent Television Commission (ITC) which replaced the old Independent Broadcasting Authority (IBA) and the Cable Authority. It is responsible for the licensing and regulation of all broadcasting in Great Britain including terrestrial, cable, satellite teletext, or local microwave distribution with the exception of services provided by the BBC or systems connecting fewer than a thousand households or a single block of flats.

Most of the most important work of the ITC is to do with the awarding and regulation of broadcasting franchises, the setting of technical standards and promotion of new methods of distribution. But for the programme makers the ITC's most important productions are probably its Programme Code and its Code of Advertising Standards and Practice. There is also a code regulating sponsorship of programmes.

The ITC Programme Code covers matters such as taste, decency, violence, privacy, impartiality, charitable appeals and religion. The programme sponsorship code sets out to protect editorial independence and provides some policing over prominent promotion of sponsors' products on screen, product placement or undue emphasis on sponsor credits. At a time when test match cricket teams wear shirts advertising rival brands of lager, and a racing car can bear the name and livery of a packet of condoms, the latter is somewhat difficult to enforce.

The ITC code on advertising largely re-states yet another code by yet another body, the Broadcasting Standards Council (see above).

The ITC does have teeth. All complaints from the public are investigated and errors of judgement can be punished. A source of bitter complaint by some broadcasters is that the ITC might go to great lengths to bring a producer to book over a single complaint about a show with an audience of millions, or because an organised pressure group is given undue attention.

In 1995 the showing on Channel 4 Television of Scorsese's

film *The Last Temptation of Christ* led to a deluge of complaints about blasphemy. On this occasion the it was noted that an identical spelling mistake in the address of the ITC appeared on every letter. The orchestrated campaign was unmasked.

The ITC may be told to drop a programme, schedule transmission at a different, usually later hour, make cuts or broadcast an apology. A company may be fined very large amounts or have the period of its licence curtailed. The ultimate sanction is the removal of a licence to broadcast. Even though the ITC has only been operative since 1991 there are political jitters about the control of television, particularly with the explosion of new networks, novel means of distribution via computer networks, the prospect of a multiplicity of digital terrestrial channels, and easy access to supposed undesirable material broadcast by or from other states of the EU.

Yet another Broadcasting Act was to have been introduced in November 1995 but was withdrawn because of a disagreement between the Department of the Environment and the Department of Trade over who was to be in charge of regulating these new commercial services. A new Broadcasting Bill is before Parliament in 1996 and new regulatory pressures are being proposed.

The Advertising Standards Authority

If your career leads you to the lush pastures of film commercials, do not feel left out. You will be subject to the control of the authorities so far described and have a code of practice of your own in addition.

The Advertising Standards Authority (ASA) was set up by the advertising industry itself, in the same spirit as the film industry set up the Board of Film Censors, to meet the need for a unified standard of content and presentation of advertisements. Its Code of Practice, although purely voluntary, is in effect enforced on television by the ITC. There are currently about 500 complaints a month about advertising, an interesting comparison with the 1000 or so a year about the actual programmes.

A lot of the complaints are about poster and print advertising rather than commercials but television advertising features prominently.

The code states that all advertisement must be:
- *legal;*
- *decent* – in this case the definition is 'not likely to give grave

or widespread offence';

- *honest* – advertisers should not play upon the credulity or ignorance of the public;
- *truthful* – advertisers may not mislead consumers by inaccuracy, ambiguity, exaggeration or otherwise.

There are a large number of specific conditions for the advertising of different categories of products such as health products, cosmetics, slimming products, mail order companies, financial services, alcoholic drinks and advertisements aimed at children.

The rules can change. All television cigarette advertising is now banned and drinks advertisements may not make a specific appeal to the young or imply a connection with sexual success. Only recently has a ban been lifted on the advertisement of sanitary towels, which raised a storm of complaints – largely from women – and the use of live models in underwear advertisements. There is great concern about the linking of children's animated cartoon programmes and advertising campaigns for associated products particularly if in the same transmission periods.

The ASA itself has few sanctions. An offending advertiser may be asked to withdraw an advertisement pending an enquiry, by which time of course the damage has been done. The ASA may ask for a public undertaking not to break the code in future. As a last resort it may ask other members of the industry not to handle productions from the offending campaign.

Harmonisation with EU law led to the Control of Misleading Advertising Regulations Act 1988 which means that in extreme cases the matter can be taken up by the Office of Fair Trading. If an advertisement is held to be blatantly misleading the Director General can apply to the courts for an injunction to prevent further publication and failure to do so would be contempt of court. The ASA may be found at the following address:

 The Advertising Standards Authority
2–16 Torrington Place
London WC1E 7HN

The British Broadcasting Corporation

The BBC predates all other broadcasting companies and has so far retained its own mechanisms for controlling programme content as well as its own financial and political relationship to the government. The history of the BBC is in part the story of the struggle against political manipulation and for financial and editorial freedom.

The BBC find themselves taking a smaller and smaller proportion of the total audience share as new services come on stream. Their income, via the licence fee, is static or even declining in real terms in the face of increasing costs, and may yet be replaced by new encryption techniques being pioneered for satellite and cable. This calls into question the very survival of the institution and there has been a need to 'keep up with the Jones's' in matters of public postures on taste and decency.

The BBC is run by a Chairman and Board of Governors appointed by the government and controlled by a licence agreement which is part of its charter. The Home Secretary has the power to order any programme not to be broadcast. This power has rarely been threatened. Control has been exercised far more effectively through the Chairman and Governors.

The day-to-day administration of the BBC is under the control of the Director General and his Board of Management. The struggle for control between the Director General and the Chairman is another theme in the history of the BBC. The BBC Charter and Licence spells out the powers and obligations of the Corporation in both general and specific terms. As a huge bureaucratic structure with its own internal checks and balances, matters of taste and decency were traditionally left to the programme makers though circumscribed by all manner of conventions for referral.

In the late 1980s the system of control became codified by the publication of a set of Producers' Guidelines and this huge volume has been progressively modified and expanded since. This must be the most comprehensive code of practice of them all. It may be purchased by outsiders and is virtually compulsory reading for anyone working for a BBC project.

Complaints were normally filtered through an internal mechanism to the heads of department concerned and dealt with locally or referred upwards. Occasionally complaints would be taken up directly by members of the Board of Governors. There is also a network of special advisory councils and regional committees though which areas of concern or complaint may be directed. Notwithstanding this, in 1994 the BBC set up its own Programme Complaints Committee on the lines of the BCC and the BSC but without superseding either of those bodies.

The numbers of complaints received have actually been declining. In the six months between April and September 1995 the BBC received 478 complaints referring to 339 items. It upheld partly or wholly 75 of the more serious amongst them. Most of these involved one-off indiscretions or the use of expletives during live transmissions on radio or television, in particular breakfast television. A number of judgements referred to the so-called 'nine o'clock watershed' before which matter suitable only for adults cannot be transmitted. The assumptions about the viewing habits of children is of course pure moonshine but the 'watershed' concept is held dear by both broadcast managements and politicians.

Only 4 per cent of the complaints received were about political bias and surprisingly perhaps, scenes of violence received only seven complaints. This was during a period in the wake of some horrific murder and abuse cases where there had been high profile discussion about the impact of explicitly violent television. In other words the public seems largely unconcerned about broadcast television standards. The agenda has moved on to the availability of pornographic and horror videotapes, illegal snuff movies and specialist satellite transmissions. The BBC, however, remains the prim and proper 'Auntie' subject to rigorous self-censorship.

Negotiations are currently underway prior to the renewal of the BBC's Charter and Agreement, due in 1996. It appears that the governors are to be told to play a more active role in advising on programmes. For the first time the Charter will spell out an obligation to show programmes 'at appropriate times' and be 'not offending to good taste and decency' or encourage crime or be offensive. As well as detailed commitments to accuracy and impartiality it must specifically avoid exploiting the susceptibilities of listeners or viewers of religious programmes. As charter renewal is taking place at the same time as the new Broadcasting Bill is due to be passed, 1996 may turn out an interesting year.

Sex and violence

With such complex systems of censorship it may seem strange that there is still political concern that programme makers need to be brought under even tighter control. The problem is in the frustrated inability of the regulators to keep up with technology.

Erotica Channel

In 1992 the first of a series of battles between the government and satellite broadcasters erupted over a subscription channel initially calling itself Red Hot Dutch which was transmitted from Holland (later from Scandinavia) and which transmitted hard pornographic material to the UK. The Home Office rushed through an order outlawing any British advertisers to use the channel and making it illegal to import or manufacture either the encryption decoders or the subscription cards.

In 1995 another Channel, Erotica TV, began transmitting hard pornography to the UK. Unlike Red Hot Dutch it was not exclusively aimed at the British market. The government has again banned the selling of British advertising and the importation of decoders or subscription cards. Unfortunately this time things may not be so simple as there is an EU Directive ensuring the freedom of information freely across borders.

The market for pornography is a lucrative one and a government committed to the idea of a free market and consumer choice at the same time as implicit censorship has found itself between a rock and a hard place. In 1995 the ITC licensed three 'soft porn' adult viewing channels. One, the Fantasy Channel, has immediately been in trouble for transmitting a film *Requiem for a Vampire*, including footage of assaults on women previously cut by the BBFC. The ITC code prohibits the showing of films not certificated in advance. Fantasy apologised, but only after threats of a £50 000 fine and their licence being revoked.

In the meantime BSkyB screened an uncut version of a film *The Killer* which was transmitted three times until the ITC intervened. BSkyB has shown itself to be rather less repentant than Fantasy.

There remains the problem that many European cable broadcasters show pornography as a matter of course. Pornography of increasing sophistication is so much a problem on the Internet that there are calls for controls not on moral grounds but to stop the system getting overloaded.

The year 1996 saw the introduction of the V-chip (viewer-controlled chip) in parts of Canada. It is envisaged that in 1998 in the USA all new TV receivers wider than 13 inches will have to have a V-chip capacity. The system entails cable and satellite transmissions carrying an encrypted signal conveying a classification of programmes similar to those of the BBFC's. The receivers are equipped with a decoding box which may be programmed to accept only chosen categories. Parents therefore will be able to screen out violent or sexual programmes in the interest of protecting their children. Even specific scenes may be blanked in mid-programme. This has aroused great interest in the UK. Apart from the administrative costs involved , the system requires viewers to invest in and program decoders. Since in most British households only the children have an idea how to program a VHS recorder, the prospects fro domestic censorship do not look bright.

Nudity advertisements

In 1994 the ITC approved an advertisement for a shower gel 'Neutralia' which showed parts of a female body being soaped. One brief shot showed a profile of a nipple.

The ITC monitored the 82 complaints received and subsequently commissioned a research survey of attitudes. Its findings have produced yet more highly detailed guidelines which accept that the naked body may sometimes be shown so long as it is relevant to the product, unclothed people are not seen touching, and men are shown only from the rear with their thighs together.

Such advertisements will be allowed only after the nine o'clock watershed which delivers such small audiences that advertisers will not rush to push back the frontiers of depravity. In this way are our morals defended.

Bad language

There is a distinction between blasphemy and bad language. Complaints about swearing or the use of words taken to be offensive still upsets members of the audience and much exercises the regulators. Bad language is less likely to be tolerated if it is used casually during a discussion or documentary even if off screen such a usage would be natural. Fashions in language change and words lose their shock value with repetition and reactions to them depend greatly on context. The word 'fuck' for example now frequently is printed in full in serious broadsheet papers and reviews but is always reduced to F*** by tabloids whose readership cannot be unused to the word. When the singer Bjork used the word in a 1995 discussion programme there were complaints, though not so many as there were when the critic Kenneth Tynan first used it on the BBC 30 years ago.

A documentary series on a platoon of soldiers in Northern Ireland removed the offensive speech and the 'bleeping' of offending words often reaches ludicrous levels with the only perceptible result of improving the lip-reading ability of the viewer. The 1995 drama series 'Jake's Progress' was able to use most taboo words in a naturalistic context including a stream of abuse from the mouth of an actress which would have brought stunned admiration from a Smithfield porter.

The programme maker must feel his or her way carefully about what is acceptable. Offensive speech is used as a matter of course in everyday contexts but might appear inappropriate in either factual or entertainment programming. The gentility of speech in soap operas like 'Eastenders' is absurd given the characterisation and story lines but is regarded as proper by much of the audience.

Blasphemy

In law the offence of blasphemy is limited to libels upon the tenets of the Christian Church and more particularly the Anglican religion. It occurs if there is an indecent description of sacred objects or outrageous comments upon holy persons or articles of faith.

It is not the views themselves but the violence of their expression which is the touchstone and only if the views are likely to lead to a breach of the peace will the law be invoked. Language may express offensive points of view but must not be scurrilous or inflammatory.

In 1923 a successful prosecution was brought against a soap box orator and pamphleteer who repeatedly outraged the religious sensibilities of passengers at Stratford East railway station. Subsequently the law lay dormant.

In 1977 the forgotten legislation was brought back to life by Mrs Mary Whitehouse, then leader of the National Viewers' and Listeners' Association, a puritanical pressure group influential between the 1960s and 1980s. A private prosecution was brought against the journal *Gay News* over a poem attributing homosexual feelings and acts to Jesus. *Gay News* was fined £1000 and the editor £500 with a suspended prison sentence of nine months.

The case did not unleash a spate of prosecutions. On the contrary it was widely stated that a law which exclusively protected the Anglican Church had no place in a plural society and that if such a law was needed it should be expanded to include all religions. Unfortunately the strongly expressed tenets of one religion are likely to be deeply blasphemous to another. The problem of definition killed the prospect of new legislation.

The issue was revived in violent circumstances when the Ayatollah Khomeini issued a Fatwah ordering Muslims to kill the British author Salman Rushdie for blasphemy against the prophet Mohammed.

British Muslims failed to invoke the existing law but found that it still only applied to Christians. They then tried another neglected law, seditious libel.

The offence of seditious libel must:

- bring into contempt the Royal Family, Government or Constitution;
- incite the public to use unlawful means to overthrow the

institutions of the state;
- raise discontent or hostility between different classes.

The case failed on the grounds that the book, *The Satanic Verses*, did not incite violence against the state nor had violence or defiance against the state resulted.

A third approach was the invocation of the Public Order Act 1987. This Act, important for programme and video makers as well as journalists, makes it an offence to publish material which is threatening, abusive or insulting or 'intends to stir up racial hatred or if racial hatred is stirred up may be stirred up thereby'. Racial hatred is defined as 'hatred against a group of persons in Great Britain defined by reference to colour, race, nationality including citizenship, or ethnic or national origins'. Matters of religion were specifically excluded.

The Muslim case failed on the grounds that they did not constitute a race or nationality (this is still being disputed on the grounds that Islam is a 'nation') and the book could not incite to violence simply because one group took exception to its contents.

It was widely asked at the time why this law was not in its turn invoked against the organisers of violent Muslim demonstration demanding the murder of a British subject.

In a secular society the problems of blasphemy are peripheral but not forgotten. In 1995 the Government clashed with the European Commission over the non-inclusion of religion in British anti-discriminatory legislation. The recent 'politically correct' concern about publishing anything which might be offensive to any group whatsoever might infect broadcasting in due course.

POSTSCRIPT

This guide has given no more than a whistle-stop tour of the problem areas that face directors, producers and other programme makers day by day. With luck it has not proved too dismal reading. If it has conveyed that there is a lot more to television production than untrammelled creative energy it will have served its purpose.

Attention to the practicalities cannot be separate from the creative input. There are plenty of low-budget programmes which look slick because of efficiently planned production, juts as there are extravagant products awash with daring effects and Hollywood-proportion sets which look like home videos put together by hyperactive 14 year olds. In the long run what counts is coming in on time and in budget without tears, as well as pleasing the audience.

The surest way to bring a brilliant career to an abrupt end is to leave a wake of ill-feeling amongst colleagues and continuing disputes with outsiders. The consequences of bad practice long outlive transmission dates, and word gets around.

Television is a very small world.

The introduction refers to the opinion of Sir John Harvey Jones that the only justification for entering a television career is the attractive lifestyle. The lifestyle is not to be sneered at. There are few other careers which can offer the same personal fulfilment, creative satisfaction, breadth of experience and sheer variety of daily work.

It is not a job for dullards, even if sadly some dullards seem to survive in it.

There was always a golden age of broadcasting and it was always the day before last. Changes which utterly depress one generation have to be seized upon as new opportunities by the next, but good professional practice changes only in the detail. If the programme maker keeps at least one eye always open for the problems described in this handbook, they need not bother him or her unduly.

Then everyone will be free to concentrate on the fascinating, demanding, real job of making television programmes.

INDEX

Lightning Source UK Ltd.
Milton Keynes UK
UKOW050255230911

179120UK00001B/56/A